Cause for Concern

Results-Oriented Cause Marketing

Stephen M. Adler

Australia · Brazil · Canada · Mexico · Singapore · Spain · United Kingdom · United States

Cause for Concern: Results-Oriented Cause Marketing
Stephen M. Adler

For more information about our products, contact us at:

Thomson Learning Academic Resource Center 1-800-423-0563

Thomson Higher Education
5191 Natorp Boulevard
Mason, Ohio 45040
USA

To Dr. Eric David Adler and Alissa Haley Adler,
the loves of my life. You have made
all the difference.

TABLE OF CONTENTS

PREFACE

For the past two decades, it has given me great joy to work with charities and corporations in such a way that both have benefited from and been enriched by the partnerships my company has been able to facilitate. Joy may seem too strong a word, but I hope this book will make it clear why it's exactly the *right* word, and why this joy has not been mine alone. Those who have shared in this work, whether their basic mission was making a profit or raising funds for others, have discovered what so many of us have long suspected: that there's more to life than money. This isn't to suggest that money isn't important. It's crucial. But to see firsthand the difference corporate giving can make to people who simply can't make it without such support is to witness a deep transformation in the human spirit.

Companies have taken a lot of knocks in the press recently, not all of them undeserved. Public perception of corporations is at a lower ebb today than it has been in many decades. No one who reads the newspapers even occasionally can have missed the seemingly endless torrent of stories about layoffs and downsizing, employees losing their pensions due to sleight-of-hand financial manipulation, consumers up in arms about product quality and increasingly distant "customer service" (how many levels do those automated phone menus have to reach before we all just give up?), and assaults on the environment that our children's children will be faced with cleaning up. Sometimes it seems as if companies just don't give a damn. But on the other hand, many companies are also skillfully aligning consumers' needs with the causes and issues they care about, and through programs at work provide vital health information on issues such as breast health and heart health and special needs such as nutrition. They also support the causes their employees care about such as conservation, safety, and affordable housing.

Of course, many companies do care. The people I've worked with in commercial organizations have been deeply concerned about the social causes they've convinced their companies to champion. And as that championship has caught fire within the company—it doesn't just happen overnight by magic—the organization as a whole has gained a new view of itself, a new sense of pride and belonging through its work with the larger community. When a company sees tangible proof of how it has made a real contribution to people outside its day-to-day competitive concerns, something like a transformation of spirit takes place. These moments of changed perspective are truly impressive and, yes, joyful.

Why then, especially in an era of rapid globalization, have so few companies committed themselves to appreciably bettering the societies in which they do business? Even those organizations that already give to social causes sometimes seem to hide their light under a bushel. Their gifts are often virtual secrets to all but those they directly benefit. Others have inherited Byzantine organizational structures that make it nearly impossible for charities to approach them. While the mechanisms *are* in place, identifying and locating the proper persons, offices, forms, and procedures can be more costly than the eventual results are worth. In some cases, these frustrations arise as the result of old and unreconstructed bureaucracies. These companies mean well, but they seem to keep getting in their own way. In other cases, the maddening paper chase is not so well meaning. Its intent is to discourage alliances with charity organizations without having to say, "Sorry, but we're just not interested."

Today, no company in its right mind should be uninterested in changing the public's view of them as arrogant, venal, and often corrupt. Whether true or false (in most cases, fortunately, they're unfounded), such assessments are very widespread these days, and extremely hard to change. Every public relations professional knows this, and winces at the implications. While companies have an unprecedented opportunity at present to turn these negative perceptions around, the necessary changes won't come about through any amount of self serving PR happy talk. In fact, far from leading to viable solutions, such empty posturing has become a major component of the very perceptions companies wish they could revise and ultimately reverse. These critical revisions and reversals are possible, but they will require something more, something that's long overdue: *a new social contract* between corporations and the societies in which they operate.

Companies need to engage not only with the profit potential of abstract markets, but with the very real problems that very real human beings face within the context of those "markets." As globalization shrinks our planet, no organization can afford to see itself as an island, unconnected to the whole. Unless corporations improve the lot of people *outside* their traditional borders, business will continue to be perceived as a less then welcome interloper in the life of the communities in which people live, work, and, not incidentally, buy products and services.

Many companies will see this as an opportunity to become more competitive and thus more profitable. And it is. However, that's not enough. The new social contract has to be motivated by a genuine sense of moral leadership—a commitment to give something back, to make a difference, to make the world a better place. Only such truly committed engagement will change minds and win hearts.

The book you are about to read is based on the work I've been involved in since I founded Charity Brands Marketing in 1985. Our vision since then has been to create mutually beneficial strategic alliances between nonprofit charities and large corporations through integrated cause-marketing partnerships.

The company has established extensive relationships with some of the world's largest and most highly respected nonprofits, including the American Heart Association, the American Diabetes Association, the American Red Cross, Easter Seals, the Humane Society of the United States, Special Olympics International, the Susan G. Komen Breast Cancer Foundation, and the National Conference on Tobacco or Health, which includes the American Cancer Society, the American Medical Association, the Centers for Disease Control and Prevention, and the American Lung Association. Previous clients have included Habitat for Humanity International, Mothers Against Drunk Driving, the Salvation Army, Second Harvest, and the March of Dimes.

Charity Brands has also developed strong relationships with some of the world's largest companies, including Aetna, American Express, AstraZeneca, AT&T Wireless, Bristol-Myers Squibb, Burger King, Capital One, Chevrolet–GM, Citigroup, Coca-Cola, Disney, Dole, FedEx, Fleet, GE, General Mills, GlaxoSmithKline, Home Depot, IBM, JC Penney, Johnson & Johnson, Kellogg's, M&M's, MasterCard, McDonald's, McGraw-Hill, Merck, Microsoft, Novartis, Parke-Davis, PepsiCo, Pfizer, Pharmacia, Procter & Gamble, Quaker

Oats, Rhone-Poulenc Rorer, Sara Lee Corporation, Sprint, Staples, Target, Walgreens, Wal-Mart, and Wyeth-Ayerst.

Despite these powerful associations, the aim of this book is not simply to recount past successes, but instead to propose and outline an entirely new way of approaching corporate marketing—one in which the fundamental needs of societies and local cultures become core values, not just feel-good brand enhancements.

I hope what you read in the following pages brings a new sense of joy to your work, just as it has to mine.

STEPHEN M. ADLER
CHARITY BRANDS MARKETING

PART I

CAUSE MARKETING PHILOSOPHY

CHAPTER 1

A BUSINESS CASE FOR CAUSE-RELATED MARKETING

Incentives to Give

Katrina, Alpha, Beta, Tsunami, Internet burst, Google, American Red Cross, United Way, Clinton Foundation, Schwarzenegger Inner City Games, and Magic Johnson Foundation all reflect the public's compassion and commitment to give. Consumers and corporations have given over $1 billion for cause-related marketing (CRM) and more than $1 trillion overall to nonprofits (NPs).

The benefits of CRM are not only limited to the increase in the greater good of local and global communities, but they also have the ability to enhance the existence of an entire corporation. As CRM expands and corporations are able to align their purposes with nonprofit organizations, they will notice an improvement in their image; the ability to deliver a better message to their customers and market differentiation; an increase in reach and sales as a result of niche marketing; and enhanced recruiting and retention abilities.

Sarbox Influence

The Sarbox influence is important to marketers in promoting the halo effect and accountability influence for CRM as well as accountability, as the following details demonstrate.

The sudden collapse of such corporate giants as Enron and World-Com revealed a disturbing pattern of corporate greed and deception that has prompted customers, investors, board members, management, and employees to question how corporate funds are spent. And that includes how funds are spent in such arenas as human rights, business ethics, environmental policies, corporate contributions, community development, and workplace issues.

Corporate governance has become a subject of interest from the lowest management ranks to the highest. The 2002 Sarbanes-Oxley

Act (Sarbox) introduced the most stringent and wide-ranging standards for corporate accountability and penalties for corporate wrongdoing ever seen in the U.S.—or anywhere else. Failure to comply can mean 25 years' imprisonment and fines up to $5 million for CEOs and board members, so we can expect directors and audit committees to closely monitor every financial outlay, including those to charities.

Audit committees will need to be certain that management has implemented an appropriate system of controls and procedures for periodic reporting. This includes both controls over the financial accounting systems and controls over completeness and accuracy of accounts presentation and disclosure. Board and audit committee members will need to focus more of their attention on appropriate checks and balances. Members must ensure that management is creating and sustaining value, even while they are being more proactive in challenging management's assumptions or recommendations.

Evidence that there is a return from support of a social cause will be something watched carefully. Companies that engage in CRM must show a return, whether it is in the form of increased sales and customer loyalty, increased employee morale and productivity, easier recruitment and retention of top talent, or all of these.

CRM is an option for today's corporations but it must be done correctly, particularly in light of Sarbox. Traditional fundraising tools like direct mail and telethons are not yielding as much "return on investment" as they once did, whereas corporations understand that they can achieve both marketing and philanthropic objectives by positioning themselves with the right CRM opportunity.

The difference lies in the nature of the program. Keep in mind that if there is no marketing objective behind or associated with the effort, then it might as well be philanthropy. Further, if it's not measured, in the way that most marketing activities are, then it might as well be philanthropy. Finally, if the program is not promoted—that is, no one knows about it—then it might as well be philanthropy.

Incidentally, while Sarbox right now does not impact nonprofit organizations or charities, there is speculation that they too will be covered by this ever-growing piece of legislation.

The mention of Sarbox is not intended to frighten but to point out not only why organizations should undertake CRM but also how to do it successfully to demonstrate a return from the effort.

Increased Competition in the Market

Companies have seen increased competition. Competitors have been suspected of financial wrongdoing and customers' attitudes towards the entire market segment is suspect. Companies have tried customer loyalty programs, relationship marketing programs, and the guru de jour's approach to marketing, but nothing seems to break through the din of messaging in the market. It is now time to deliver a message with passion and commitment. Deliver a message in a forum where companies share some of the values of customers. A well planned and executed CRM strategy can accomplish just this.

CRM is a strategy employed to build a better relationship with a company's core customers through a cooperative effort with a charitable organization that shares the company's customer base. CRM can create a halo effect, improve brand image, increase sales, provide money for charities, and leverage the asset base of a partnership of both charities and businesses.

Consumers may prefer to do business with a company that stands for something beyond profits, but that, combined with the emotional fulfillment that comes from philanthropy, may not be enough to justify the investment of staff and money in a charity or other social cause. Embracing the cause must make good business sense. Pure philanthropy may be questionable to investors and other stakeholders who are dependent on corporate profits to live.

CRM, on the other hand, enables an organization to embrace a cause and also achieve marketing and other objectives. The objectives that CRM helps organizations achieve are vast and varied, and are thus both desirable programs that lead to great success.

Changing Public Attitudes—Image

CRM is desirable to corporations because it can increase sales volume and establish a theme for promotion with a retailer, such as Children's Miracle Network at Wal-Mart. It can also leverage public and government support through established times of year such as Black History

Month, American Heart Month, and National Safety Week, among many others. Programs share success through reach and revenue by leveraging celebrities who support their causes, such as Arnold Schwarzenegger's After School All Stars, Magic Johnson's Foundation Technology Centers, Dan Marino's Foundation for Autism, and Katie Couric's cofounding of the National Colorectal Cancer Research Alliance (NCCRA). Reach is achieved through public service announcements (PSAs), video news releases, and celebrity interviews, which create cohesiveness for the cause and the corporate brand.

Earlier, the current state of trust in American companies was mentioned and the impact that CRM can have on this trust factor. Research shows that consumers will reward those businesses that demonstrate a genuine commitment to philanthropy. In the Business in the Community Study in the UK (http://www.bitc.org.uk), consumers reported as follows:

- 83% "I have a more positive image of a company that supports a cause."
- 78% "I'd be more likely to buy a product supporting a cause."
- 66% "I'd switch brands to support a cause."
- 62% "I'd switch retailers to support a cause."
- 54% "I'd pay more for a product that supports a cause."
- 50% "I remember buying a product with a cause overlay."
- 87% of employees at companies with cause programs feel a strong sense of loyalty to their employer (versus 67% of employees at companies with no such program).

Corporate experience has been that CRM programs increase sales. As important to the bottom line, CRM initiatives build customer loyalty that has a long-term impact on corporate profitability. Consumers appear to be drawn to companies that are associated with a social cause or issue. Corporate alignment with nonprofit groups in the development of product marketing and promotion has provided windfalls for both organizations. These windfalls are the result of public perceptions that they are getting more quality for their purchase when they are helping a given cause, or the community at large, as with the American Express "Charge Against Hunger" campaign. CRM also can undo negative connotations associated with a brand. This is why liquor and tobacco companies often associate themselves with causes to minimize the disrepute associated with their industry. Likewise, brands that are seen to possess a very commercial and greedy image have been known to develop a better image, showing a softer, nicer, more humane side, by entering into a CRM relationship.

Finally, brands that plan to approach the investment market for raising money from the public often show the warm side of their personality via a CRM effort. Investors who are not doing extensive research on the brand may invest because they believe a brand with good intentions can be trusted.

That the public cares about the social responsibility assumed by companies is behind the founding in 2002 of Companies That Care, a national, not-for-profit organization to encourage, celebrate, and sustain businesses and organizations that are committed to ongoing community service. The newest additions to this organization are Baxter Credit Union, The Care of Trees, CHAN Healthcare Auditors, Convergint Technologies LLC, Delnor-Community Health System, FPL Group, Grant Thornton LLP, Health Grades, KPMG LLP, Office Depot, Opto Technology, PJV Interconnection, Rauland-Borg Corporation, TAP Pharmaceutical Products, The Supply Room Companies, Triangle Printers, and University Health System Consortium. According to Business in the Community, to become honored, these companies must consistently demonstrate the following ten characteristics:

1. Sustain a work environment founded on dignity and respect for all employees
2. Make employees feel their jobs are important
3. Cultivate the full potential of all employees
4. Encourage individual pursuit of work/life balance
5. Enable the well-being of individuals and families through compensation, benefits, policies, and practices
6. Develop great bosses who excel at managing people as well as results
7. Appreciate and recognize the contributions of people who work there
8. Establish and communicate standards for ethical behavior and integrity

9. Get involved in community endeavors and/or public policy
10. Consider the human toll when making business decisions

Some companies—for example, Phillip Morris—had traditionally supported social issues such as the arts and human rights for many years. But, until being practically forced by the government to deal with underage smoking, they did not visibly address smoking-as-a-problem issues publicly. This campaign, however, actually had a reverse effect on its targeted audience. A study commissioned by an anti-smoking foundation found that it led to an increase in teen smoking. "Philip Morris should pull its ads off the air at once," American Legacy Foundation President and CEO Cheryl Healton said. "It should call an immediate halt to a campaign that not only doesn't work but actually harms the very kids it purports to help" (Newsday 5/29/02). This demonstrates the need for a company to analyze and align its message before reaching its targeted audience.

Other companies with a progressive view and multiyear CRM planning cycles include Bristol-Myers Squibb, AstraZeneca, and Merck—all members of the American Heart Association Pharmaceutical Roundtable, which offers marketing benefits that have helped increase revenues for their relevant brands, including, respectively, Pravachol, Crestor, and Mevacor. Kmart has attained great reach and revenue from its ten-year relationship with the March of Dimes, which resulted in increased revenue and great employee goodwill.

Two other examples include Walgreens's monumental effort and competition with their stores and employees with the American Heart Month and American Cancer Society "Hope Blooms with You" retail programs. These programs were designed by great visionaries, Ed King and Dan Murray at Walgreens. The second great multiyear program linked Habitat for Humanity and The Home Depot. This program, which resulted in thousands of new homes for those in need, leveraged Jimmy Carter as a spokesperson and resulted in great benefit to Habitat for Humanity and all of the suppliers to The Home Depot. The program has also evolved into a multisite program and has leveraged with other sponsors, including Lowe's and the Whirlpool Corporation.

Market Differentiation

Given the competitive marketplace, CRM can help address a fundamental issue: Today, marketing challenges that once seemed insurmountable are no longer so. Ten-year planning horizons were replaced with five-year planning horizons, only to be replaced by three-year planning timetables. A new catchword, "hyper competition," has appeared. Traditional sustainable advantage was dead, because competition always has the potential to outmaneuver an incumbent with an established position. Growth appeared a lot more difficult in a zero-economic profit world.

CRM is a way around this. It can both defend against another company and also extend your organization's competitive advantage and the continual creation of new advantages.

At this point, a strategist seeking long-term growth basically has two options: (1) implement initiatives that extend and defend an established position, and/or (2) launch new initiatives with the potential to create new positions of advantage. Both options can be addressed by integrating CRM into the strategy, or using CRM as the strategy itself.

Companies can separate themselves from their competitors by demonstrating a social conscience through CRM. Think of McDonald's sponsorship of Ronald McDonald House, or American Express's effort to alleviate world hunger, or Pfizer donating its AIDS drug fluconazole to South Africa. Each of these organizations stands out because it didn't rely solely on traditional advertising.

Visa reported a 17 percent increase in sales during its November/December 1997 "Reading Is Fundamental" campaign, compared to sales in the same months in 1996. Similarly, a BMW campaign associated with eradicating breast cancer, in which driving test cars generated a $1 per mile charitable donation, reportedly resulted in sales of hundreds more vehicles. And Wendy's International reported an increase in jumbo fry sales in Denver by more than a third when it contributed a portion of each purchase to Denver's Mercy Medical Center.

Price doesn't seem to be an issue. A British study reported that almost two-thirds of consumers said they were willing to pay more for a product associated with a good cause. And nearly two-thirds of consumers reported that when price and quality are good, they would be more likely to switch brands or retailers to one associated with a good cause. Given the great difficulties that face businesses in the constant battle to maintain margins, this should be music to a brand manager's ears. According to The Home Depot, "Our customers trust us to help them make repairs to their home, and they trust us to be responsible to the community" (Meyer).

The Home Depot has discovered its positive reputation comes in handy when opening new stores. The home improvement chain's extensive community activities build goodwill, a priceless commodity that can counter bad publicity and often aid companies in meetings with public officials. The company believes that if it can tell its story about its commitment to local communities, it has an easier time getting government approvals for new sites.

And we can't forget Timberland, the Stratham, NH-based producer of high-quality outdoor apparel, footwear, and accessories. It enhances its brand—and its bond with customers—by offering them chances to volunteer. "Part of the way Timberland is building a more in-depth relationship with customers is by offering not just an opportunity for a product transaction but for a relationship that takes into account community wealth and value" (Meyer), according to Ken Freitas, Timberland's vice president of social enterprise.

There is no question that CRM has a positive effect on corporate reputation. With recent financial scandals eroding public trust, it is now more crucial than ever for companies to pay attention to how they are viewed by the larger community. Companies must be much more diligent in their actions and communications to improve and maintain their positive image.

For many companies, CRM has helped them to create an alternative and distinctive approach to brand advertising. In a marketplace with a considerable number of similar products, CRM can help companies distinguish themselves from their peers by offering the consumer the opportunity to contribute to something more than a company's bottom line, which seems to have a greater value today both nationally and locally. Indeed, even international brands can better identify with local markets by linking themselves with community organizations or with regional or community chapters of nongovernmental organizations (NGOs).

As more and more companies use CRM campaigns, an ever-increasing number of consumers are accepting them as a means of making purchase decisions. In the UK, a study found that 88 percent of consumers were aware of cause marketing programs and 77 percent said that such programs had positively changed their behavior.

Niche Marketing—Increased Reach/Sales

Locally, companies have found that partnering with NPs can help them connect with specific demographic or geographic markets. For instance, by partnering with Susan G. Komen Breast Cancer Foundation in support of the Foundation's "Race for the Cure" events, Ford Motor Company successfully positioned itself among a formerly disinterested target market—women car buyers.

In addition to its substantial financial and in-kind donations to Race events, Ford has provided millions of media impressions in the form of paid advertisements and/or "leveraged" PSAs from its media vendors. Not only has this communicated a critical health message to women, but it has linked the cause to its brand.

Creating a niche for your organization via CRM isn't easy. You will need to know your competition. Look not only at their interests but also at their size, scope of services, and geographic areas they serve. Once you have accumulated this information, you need to ask yourself what your organization might be able to do to increase its visibility in the industry by standing out from the others.

In conducting this evaluation, you must also identify and agree on who the stakeholders of the organization are and/or who the organization would like them to be. Such a self-evaluation should help you determine whether or not you are embodying your desired image and, if not, what changes are necessary.

Such an analysis shouldn't be limited to marketing staff. Gauge all internal staff's understanding of the organization's image, as more often than not it is the internal staff that represents the public face of the organization.

Once this analysis is done, use your findings to determine your cause-related mission. Keep in mind to set rules by which your organization will thereafter be publicly visible. Ensure that they are used through all segments and services of the organization and serve to focus on the organization and position it for public recognition.

None of this is easy, but those organizations with successful CRM programs demonstrate it is necessary. Integration of the branding concepts tied to CRM needs to be incorporated into all segments of your organization—from corporate stationery and business cards to website design and fund-raising thank-you notes.

Don't allow divergence from your guidelines. Owning your space in an issue is difficult—anticipate that it will take time, money, and sometimes some significant event or campaign. But remember, if your organization focuses its efforts to communicate in a consistent and meaningful manner, first to stakeholders and ultimately to the general public, you will have carved out an "ownable" space via CRM.

Recruitment, Retention, and Cause-Related Marketing

So far, we have been looking at the impact of CRM on your marketing effort. But the experiences of socially conscious organizations have demonstrated that CRM efforts can enable companies to compete successfully to attract and keep top performers. In one study, 85 percent of U.S. executives said that one of the most important long-term objectives of CRM programs was to increase employee loyalty. This is going to be very important in the years to come.

Over the last half of the 1990s, much was written and discussed about the so-called war for talent and the problems employers had in retaining and engaging skilled, young, more diverse workers. The economic downturn of the early 2000s stopped this talk and in some cases reversed it. Instead of a concern for retention and engagement, the talk quickly turned to downsizing and separation. Was the experience of the latter half of the 1990s a true long-term trend or just a bump in the road?

After careful study, it appears that the war for talent is not a short-term phenomenon but the beginning of a true, long-term change in the labor force. This is because the factors that were driving the events in the last half of the 1990s are still present today and they're predicted to stay for another 15 years.

The Coming Labor Shortage

Employers think that they are going to have plenty of workers forever, but that is not so. The buyer's market in which employers find themselves as of 2006 is temporary. Maybe it will last another year or two. After that, experts warn, companies will be back in the same predicament as in 1999 and 2000. One day in the not-too-distant future, job seekers will have the advantage. When that happens, the effect on some organizations—particularly those that have let employee engagement and retention strategies take a back seat to seemingly more pressing issues of corporate survival—could be severe.

According to a 2000 Bureau of Labor Statistics report, by 2008 there could be as many as 5 to 6.2 million more jobs than there are employees in the United States, 7 to 10 million by 2010, and an astounding 21 to 40 million by 2015. According to Jeff Taylor, founder of the online job marketplace monster.com, the troubles employers had in hiring in 1999 will be "only a footprint for what we'll see in 2008. We'll be facing the worst labor shortage in our lifetime" (Michelman).

Companies will have to bend over backward to retain skilled workers, lure skilled retirees back into the labor force, or re-deploy other workers. Eventually, the demand will be met. But at what cost? Employees will definitely have the upper hand in this labor market.

Retention in the Future

What employers will do to counter the future labor shortages is not difficult to predict: Most will wait until there is a burning platform and then will bid up wages; raid competitors for employees; induce older workers to stay on the job; outsource whatever work they can; and, perhaps, while not ignoring the post-9-11 climate we live in, lobby the government to increase the quota for skilled immigrants.

Fortunately, there are actions that companies can take today to build a culture that engages and retains the best and brightest.

There are many factors of importance that you probably already appreciate—for instance, a solid frontline management team that will provide open and honest information on the organization's mission, policies, systems, and practices. Employees will want supervisors who treat them with respect and dignity. They will want supervisors to be coaches, mentors, and teachers. They will want supervisors to provide instant feedback, lots of positive reinforcement, and a lot of pats on the back. They will want managers who inspire and motivate them, create a passion for the work they do, and do a lot of one-on-one communication.

Employees will also want good training opportunities to increase their marketable skills. They will ask for challenging work that contributes value. They will also want task variety. If the half-life of the skills needed to perform the job is long, employees want a lot more task variety, primarily to avoid boredom and to have more lines on their resume when they are forced to get another job. On the other hand, if the half-life of the skill is short (e.g., engineering), they do not want a lot of task variety. They want a lot of experience in their narrow field so they can stay up to speed in their ever-changing occupation.

They will want a positive work culture. And related to that, they will want pride in their organization. They will want to work in organizations that demonstrate a community spirit, which certainly includes CRM.

Timberland is only one of many organizations with CRM efforts that have discovered the people benefits of their cause-related efforts. More than 80 percent of Timberland's employees take advantage of a generous policy offering 40 paid hours annually to volunteer for one of the organization's environmental activities.

Avon, which relies on 480,000 independent sales reps to market beauty products in the U.S., has found its breast cancer education and early-detection program motivates both the customers and the "Avon Ladies." Last year, when it was announced at a national convention of 6,000 sales reps how much money had been raised for breast cancer programs, which according to the Avon Foundation was more than $400 million worldwide, a roar of cheers rose up from the room.

And The Home Depot, which has to hire around 2,000 new workers weekly, says its social-cause efforts enable it to do this. The organization's affordable housing, at-risk youth, environmentalism, and disaster preparedness and relief programs are all paying dividends with recruits. And, once aboard, the company reports, employees aren't likely to leave. The company's turnover is considerably lower than the industry average.

Indeed, employees attracted to CRM relationships exhibit tremendous morale, loyalty, and job performance.

Thus, a business case can be made for CRM. In an era of increasing competition and heightened public scrutiny of corporate activities, you should recognize the power of CRM to help you gain favor not only among employees and current and prospective customers but also investors and government agencies.

CHAPTER 2

BUILDING YOUR BUSINESS' CASE FOR CAUSE-RELATED MARKETING

It is no secret that many major corporations are finding it increasingly difficult to build their brands and engender customer loyalty. There are numerous reasons for this, and some of the more important ones are explored in the following pages.

Corporate scandals . . . a public saturated by ads . . . the Internet— the end result of these trends is that corporations are finding it increasingly difficult to create advertising campaigns that speak to vast numbers of individuals in an increasingly diverse society. When analyzing the power of CRM and its benefits, one must keep in mind the needs of their particular company and the solutions that CRM offers:

Need	Solution
Image problem	Enhanced reputation through CRM
Hyper competition	Product differentiation, competitive advantage
Inefficient access to markets	Leverage nonprofit partners to reach niches
Poor branding	Effective brand placement
Customer retention	Build customer loyalty
Employee turnover	Build employee loyalty

Image

CRM offers the ability to relate to diverse individuals because it is well suited to the American psyche overall. The general public likes to reward companies that demonstrate a genuine commitment to philanthropy. In a recent study, consumers responded as shown in Figure 1.

Figure 1

Consumer Sentiments Toward CRM

Statement	Response Rate
"I have a more positive image of a company that supports a cause."	83%
"I'd be more likely to buy a product supporting a cause."	78%
"I'd switch brands to support a cause."	66%
"I'd pay more for a product that supports a cause."	62%
"I remember buying a product with a cause overlay."	50%

Source: The 2004 Cone Corporate Citizenship Study, Boston, MA.

The implications of the above chart are threefold:

1. Traditional brand building tactics seem to be losing their effectiveness.
2. CRM is critical to building customer loyalty.
3. Savvy companies must use a combination of traditional and cause-related marketing tactics to achieve their goals.

Consumers are willing to put their money where their heart is and will switch brands if a competitor supports philanthropic activities that more closely match their values.

Community Support

It's painfully obvious that the media and the general public have no patience or compassion for corporate malfeasance. And while no amount of CRM will blunt the wrath of a government prosecutor, establishing strong ties with the local community may help a company survive missteps and mistakes with their brand image intact. Think of CRM as an insurance policy that can be cashed in during a crisis.

When polled in the 2000 Cone/Roper Executive Study, 87 percent of executives said that they felt that gaining community support was another important long-term objective of CRM programs.

Alignment of Purpose

While marketers may lament the death of mass marketing, cause-related marketers have seen this as an opportunity to rebuild consumer trust and to align their companies with oft-ignored and hard-to-reach customer segments. CRM is the perfect tool for today's marketplace, allowing corporations to show that they "walk the walk" and bond with new market segments that they would have been unable to reach with traditional marketing techniques.

Market Differentiation

In a market filled with "me-too" goods, CRM can help companies distinguish themselves from their peers by this enticing proposition: The purchase of your company's product makes a difference in your world.

This proposition also allows international brands to build bridges and bond with local markets. All a company needs to do is to link itself with local organizations, or with regional or community chapters of NGOs that are actively involved in the community, and take an active role in their efforts.

Save the Children provides an example of an international organization that uses a restaurant chain, Denny's, for powerful placement throughout its U.S. restaurants and through a branded merchandise program.

Another example of a company that links itself effectively with charitable organizations is Tupperware. Tupperware bonds with children throughout the United States through its affiliation with the Boys & Girls Clubs of America. It bonds internationally through its affiliation with the SOS Children's Villages in France and the Baltic Regions, and its affiliation with the Boys and Girls Clubs in both Canada and Japan. These affiliations, as well as several others, create a powerful interest for the Tupperware Children's Foundation.

Improved Messaging

With public perception of corporations at an all-time low and consumers being bombarded with hundreds of advertisements every day, the American public has grown distrustful of traditional brand-building vehicles. Anecdotal evidence of this has been the number of pundits pronouncing the demise of the 30-second television spot.

Marketing and media moguls such as Jim Stengel and Bernard Glock of Procter & Gamble (P&G) have taken specific note of the new trends of consumers, and Larry Light, director of McDonald's marketing, has said that the decrease in effectiveness of mass marketing such as the 30-second television spot is "the end of brand positioning as we know it."

As technology continues to progress, and communication channels continue to expand, the marketplace becomes full of static, and the masses become increasingly more difficult to reach. A number of trends also are making it incredibly difficult for corporations to get their message out.

Although the use of demographic analysis and target marketing allowed advertisers to create custom messages to specific audiences, this has caused tremendous fragmentation in the marketplace. Additional fragmentation has occurred with the use of the Internet as a marketing tool, which has allowed companies to define and target specific micro-markets.

For example, in 2005, P&G announced that it would cut its television expenditures and increase its Internet advertising expenditures— a clear signal that targeted Internet purchases geared to micro-markets were quickly gaining ground on the 30-second television spots aimed at mass markets.

The digital future project also discovered that the number of hours spent on the Internet surpassed the number of hours spent watching television in 2003. This, in combination with the effect that of digital video recording devices such as TiVo that allow viewers to skip 30-second television spots, has left marketers in a situation they have never before faced.

A recent Business in the Community consumer research study entitled *Profitable Partnerships* reports that consumer response to CRM is not restricted to the United States. A study in the United Kingdom found that 88 percent of consumers were aware of cause marketing programs and 77 percent said that such programs had positively changed their behavior.

The facts point to a simple conclusion: Instead of pouring money into traditional advertising campaigns, companies need to think more strategically. And all roads lead to CRM as a mandatory component in any outreach effort.

Niche Marketing

Many companies have found that partnering with NPs can help them create a relationship with a specific demographic or penetrate geographic markets.

One company that has excelled in this arena is Ford Motor Company. By partnering with the Susan G. Komen Breast Cancer Foundation's Race for the Cure events, Ford was able to create traction with women car buyers (a market segment that was notoriously hard to reach and interest). In addition to its substantial financial and in-kind donations to Race events, Ford issued thousands of public service announcements.

The end result of this: Not only was Ford able to communicate a critical health message to women, but it also was able to link its brand to a high-profile cause—something that should yield considerable benefits for years to come.

Ford's success triggered other reactions as well. BMW quickly followed with the "Drive for the Cure," which we, Charity Brands Marketing created. "Drive for the Cure" asked women to take a test drive and bring their spouses to share in the joy of giving, because for each mile driven, BMW donates $1 to to the Susan G. Komen Breast Cancer Foundation. In its 12-year existence, it has raised over $15 million. It has also been enhanced and is now called "The Ultimate Drive."

This CRM program was a powerhouse of essential elements: a great charity, a great luxury brand, and a committed volunteer organization of cancer survivors who were willing to drive BMW automobiles from dealer to dealer, creating local commitment, interest, and power.

Recruitment and Retention

CRM goes far beyond a company's ability to compete in the marketplace and create brand loyalty; it also affects employee morale. The Cone Roper Survey of cause-related trends mentioned earlier also reports that 87 percent of employees at companies with CRM programs felt a stronger sense of loyalty to their employer (versus 67 percent of employees at companies with no such program).

CRM may bring a number of intangible benefits. Anecdotal evidence suggests that socially active companies may see enhanced morale, improved productivity, and employee loyalty. Senior management across the United States certainly believes this to be true: 85 percent of U.S. executives said that one of the most important long-term objectives of CRM programs was to increase employee loyalty.

An obvious conclusion suggests itself. Socially active companies will enjoy increased brand loyalty, a stronger competitive position and improved messaging vehicle, an increase in sales, and improved recruiting and retention rates. Those that are not socially active will lose market share to their charitably inclined competitors.

A number of facts prove that increasing numbers of corporations are recognizing that CRM is a business imperative. In 2001—a year in which most marketing budgets were slashed—spending on cause sponsorships in the U.S. and Canada increased 5 percent from the previous year ($696.35 million to $733 million).

According to the Cone Roper Survey, 91 percent of marketing executives and senior individuals at philanthropic foundations believed that CRM enhanced corporate or brand reputation. The respondents of the consumer survey indicated that when price and quality were equal, two-thirds would switch brands or retailers to one associated with a good cause.

A reason for the interest in CRM is the recognition of the needs that it satisfies, especially from the corporations' perspective. In order to observe the importance of CRM, it is essential to be aware of the specific needs that it not only addresses but can satisfy.

Wrapping It Up

The benefits of CRM are numerous and significant. Once the corporation and the nonprofit's goals are aligned properly, a CRM campaign helps a company

- Create product loyalty
- Align precisely with specific target markets
- Build brand awareness
- Bond with hard-to-reach audiences
- Capitalize on the trend toward market fragmentation
- Differentiate commodity products from competitors
- Enhance recruitment and retention efforts
- Generate support in the community

In these competitive times, companies need every means at their disposal to maximize their chances for fiscal success. Considering the numerous benefits brought by CRM and the decreasing effectiveness of traditional marketing vehicles, it is clear that most businesses will find it to be one of the most powerful tools in their marketing toolbox.

CHAPTER 3

WIN/WIN PHILOSOPHIES FOR CAUSE-RELATED MARKETING PARTNERSHIPS

Successful CRM partnerships that tend to flourish are ones in which the corporation's and the nonprofit's goals, values, and mission are aligned. When these criteria are met, the business is able to leverage its competencies within the context of the relationship, and the outreach effort speaks to customers' needs, interests, and values.

CRM relationships have the potential to become long-lasting. Corporate sponsor American Express and nonprofit Share Our Strength's "Charge Against Hunger" campaign (1993–1996) is one such example. Since CRM relationships are expanding currently and can become enduring endeavors, companies must choose their partners wisely.

Bob Speltz, global grant manager at Nike, has developed a checklist for selecting partners for his company. In addition to being professional, dynamic, and flexible, they should have

- Experience in the design and execution of national grant-making programs
- Credibility with key stakeholders
- A national reputation
- A commitment to true partnership
- Experience in working with celebrities and a Fortune 500 company

Creating Perfect Partnerships

Once you have compiled and completed a checklist like that of Speltz for your company, it is time to find the perfect NP for your CRM initiative. Use the following guidelines to help you identify potential partners and put the newly formed relationship on a firm foundation. The first four points specifically adhere to identifying the proper partner, while the last three specifically address how to make the aligned partnership a success:

1. *Determine if the corporation's and the nonprofit's cultures are aligned.* Some companies position themselves as innovative and daring. Think Apple Computer. Other corporations use trust and credibility as the foundation of their brand platform. Think large banks and brokerage houses.

This also holds true for NPs. People for the Ethical Treatment of Animals and Greenpeace are two organizations that are renowned for dramatic gestures to attract the attention of the general public. The National Anti-Vivisection Society and the National Parks and Conservation Association, conversely, are known for a much more studied and conservative approach.

When creating your short list of partners, winnow out organizations whose ethos do not match yours. You do not want to pick a partner that could create brand dissonance or other problems, but rather one that is a natural extension of your corporate culture and values.

One simple question can help you eliminate potential candidates: Would you employ analogous strategies and tactics used by the NP at your firm? If you answer no, then it's probably best to look for a better-suited partner.

An apt illustration of aligned cultures is the pairing of GlaxoSmithKline (GSK), a research-based pharmaceutical company that aims to assist in the positive growth of an ever-evolving healthcare environment, with the American Heart Association (AHA) a national voluntary health agency dedicated to reducing disability and death from cardiovascular diseases and stroke. Their collaborative efforts have been a great success.

Hill's Pet Nutrition and the Humane Society of the United States provides another example of successfully aligned cultures. Hill's Pet Nutrition strives to make the highest-quality pet nutrition available, and make a difference to people and their pets, while the Humane Society of the United States tries to improve the lives of animals here at home and worldwide.

2. Identify differences between the corporation's and the nonprofit's culture.
The old saying that no two people are the same certainly holds
true for organizations: Every one has its own culture and values.
Instead of letting these differences remain unspoken or become
trivialized, it is important to have key stakeholders identify
potential flashpoints and areas of disagreement. Bringing these
issues to light at the beginning should help you more easily
address challenges during the course of the relationship.

3. Get to know each other.
As CRM efforts are high-profile undertakings, they can yield
significant benefits. But with any public initiatives, failures can be
equally as dramatic. Make sure that you have several face-to-face
meetings with your partner before entering into a formal agreement. These meetings will build trust between the two organizations, which should contribute to superior implementation and
execution of the undertaking.

4. Set clear expectations.
CRM efforts can be complicated. Special events, fundraising
activities, and PSAs are just a few examples of the activities you
and your partner may sponsor. Every initiative, however, will likely
require significant human power and resources to bring it to
fruition.

   Right from the start, clearly define roles and expectations for
each partner. By doing this, you will minimize the chance for
misunderstanding and let your partner know what resources will
be available for these outreach efforts.

5. Create an internal team.
Now that you have set expectations, create a team at your
company with individuals from all of the departments that will
be involved in the CRM efforts. Generally speaking, you'll
probably want to have individuals from accounting, advertising,
community relations, human resources, marketing, and public
relations.

   Share with your team the benefits of CRM (see Chapter 2 for
a list). Help them understand how this effort will benefit the

company, the customer, the community, and themselves. This
will create a sense of ownership and motivation and also increase
the chances that the partnership will succeed.

A number of companies have benefited a great deal as a result
of their involvement in CRM partnerships. For example, SUBWAY
Restaurants experienced a double-digit increase in sales as a
result of their lower-fat menu that worked in conjunction with
the American Heart Association. General Mills attributed their
4 percent increase in sales to their involvement with the AHA and
their "Healthy Breakfast" campaign. American Express also
reported a 28 percent card usage increase during their sponsorship
of the restoration of the Statue of Liberty in the mid-1980s.

6. Develop communication strategies.
Your new partner and your internal team should now meet to
develop communication strategies and tactics that capitalize on
each party's core strengths. Craft campaigns and tactics that will
involve and motivate key constituents, and, if possible, the general
public.

7. Set benchmarks.
Although some of the benefits of CRM are clearly intangible,
such as enhanced goodwill in the community, many other aspects
of the program can be quantifiable. Just as you would with most
activities at your corporation, set realistic benchmarks in order to
determine if the campaign is achieving its goals, and if not, what
steps should be taken to improve its performance.

"Perfect Partnerships"

Numerous instances in the CRM world already exist where corporations and nonprofits were essentially perfect partners. The following
examples provide several campaigns, communication strategies, and
tactics used by various successful partnerships:

- The pairing of Johnson & Johnson with Dr. C. Everett Koop for
  the "Safe Kids Campaign" benefited both BAND-AID and other
  Johnson & Johnson health brands. This partnership was a logical
  tie that brought a positive view to the brand and its image. Dr.

Koop is a renowned former surgeon general who added a great
deal of trust and esteem to the Johnson & Johnson brand.

- SUBWAY with its "7 under 6" sandwiches, tied in with the
AHA's Heart Walk. This helped the chain improve its image and
gain the halo effect of the AHA.
- Arnold Schwarzenegger, as chairman of the President's Coun-
cil of Physical Fitness and Sports, forged a partnership with
Procter & Gamble, which demonstrated a win-win partnership
between families and health.
- During his presidency, Bill Clinton participated in Safe Start.
This program was designed to educate American consumers
about safe driving practices. This logical partnership was
launched by the National Safety Council.
- The American Heart Association, American Cancer Society, and
March of Dimes launched the Triple Play Program with the
Florida Department of Citrus, which stressed the health benefits
in orange juice, fresh grapefruit, and grapefruit juice.
- Walgreens, in cooperation with the American Cancer Society,
launched "Hope Blossoms with You," a pin-up program that
united employees and stores for the American Cancer Society.
They followed up with a program for the AHA in February,
which is National Heart Month.
- The Ford Motor Company initiated Ford Force, a program
where dealers in the United States joined to raise money for
breast cancer research.
- The American Red Cross launched an online program with
Microsoft called "Together We Can Save a Life." [clear] This
was a public awareness campaign that targeted a new generation
of blood donors, stressing how vital their donations were to
others.
- Donald Trump, Don King, and Avril Lavigne offered items on
eBay, such as lunch with them and free guitar lessons, in order
to raise money for charities.
- MBNA launched a partnership with the Humane Society of the
United States. A credit card was created to benefit the Humane
Society and help consumers who love pets for this great
organization.

- Procter & Gamble, Kimberly Clark, Scott, Nabisco, and over 50 manufacturers launched series of free standing insert programs for the Children's Miracle Network to help Children's Hospitals worldwide.

While these examples were great successes, and the specific guidelines described earlier in the chapter outline how to go about identifying and creating good potential partnerships, with the growth of CRM, new trends are emerging. These trends can also assist you in finding the right organization with whom to enter into a cause-related partnership.

Trends in Cause-Related Partnerships

As CRM has made its way into the mainstream of corporate America, three distinct types of partnerships have emerged.

- *Regionalizing:* Some companies have taken a regional approach in their CRM activities. They "think local and act local," and this can yield real benefits.

    For instance, Ford Motor Company participated in a partnership developed with the American Heart Association Heritage Affiliate. In their "Chefs with Heart" event, Ford and the AHA were able to target individuals in New York, New Jersey, and Connecticut when 20 of the best New York chefs cooked their best recipes and Ford Dealers of Manhattan lined the sidewalk in front of the entrance to the Peninsula Hotel with Jaguars, Thunderbirds, and the rest of their great fleet. This event was a win for all in the tri-state region.

    Group Health Insurance (GHI) wanted to reach the same tri-state area consumers. In order to do this, they used regional buses and metro north advertisement space and participated in a program that also helped the American Heart Association Heritage Affiliate. The campaign reached consumers in the region with high-level impressions.

    Banks in New York have also regionalized their marketing through the use of Affinity products. Chase Bank has been particularly innovative in CRM by donating portions of its ATM fees to regional nonprofits and charities.

- *Internationalizing:* While some companies are looking no further than their proverbial backyard for partners, global concerns are seeking NPs with an international reach.

UNICEF, the International Federation of the Red Cross and Red Crescent Societies, and Amnesty International are all NPs with an international reach. In fact, UNICEF has crafted its own guidelines for working with the business community. The willingness of the company to exercise corporate social responsibility and brand values are central in their search for the best ally and alliance. They engage with various corporations on a variety of levels, seeking to advance their mission of ensuring the health, education, and equality of every child. UNICEF's notably successful international partnerships exist with corporations such as IKEA, Montblanc, Orange Telecommunications, and the Association of Tennis Professionals (ATP).

The International Federation of Red Cross and Red Crescent Societies is the world's largest humanitarian organization. Its aim is to mobilize the power of humanity to improve the lives of vulnerable people, often those caught up in natural disasters, those suffering in poverty brought about by socio-economic crises, refugees, and victims of health emergencies. The organization is specifically needed in times of utmost emergency, like the 2004 tsunami. The unparalleled natural disaster that stuck Southeast Asia in December 2004 showed the world the value of and need for global nonprofit organizations. The expanse reach and various causes in which global NPs are involved make them easy organizations with which to find a common thread and not only reinforce corporate and brand image, but also to make a positive contribution to some of the most desperate individuals at the most crucial time. PG&E Corporation and State Farm Insurance, as well as many other national corporations, have been recent sponsors of the Red Cross and Red Crescent Societies.

Amnesty International is a worldwide movement of people who campaign for internationally recognized human rights.

Recent sponsors and donors have included companies such as Amazon, MTV, and Asterisk Entertainment.

- *Leveraging with Existing Partners:* Instead of struggling to create a CRM campaign in saturated markets, some companies are partnering with other corporations as a way to gain quick entry and to make a difference in the community.

  The credit card company Visa once partnered with Kmart in a CRM effort to benefit anti-drug education. Visa made a contribution based on the number of Visa transactions at Kmart stores. Kmart has been particularly aggressive with the March of Dimes and their birth defect prevention efforts. Former chair Joe Antinori was especially active in mobilizing consumers and using the leverage of the corporate CEO in a top-down approach with employees, consumers, and vendors.

  More recently, Timberland created the Red Boot campaign to raise funding and awareness for its nonprofit partner City Year through sales of a special collection of apparel, accessories, and footwear bearing both partners' logos.

  The Home Depot has also partnered with Habitat for Humanity by encouraging their vendors to donate raw materials to construction projects. In turn, these vendors receive enhanced placement and association with Habitat for Humanity in Home Depot store locations. I personally was on a Home Depot build with Jimmy Carter and presidents of many Home Depot divisions. The partnership with Habitat for Humanity was unprecedented in that every vendor in the store participated in this serious CRM partnership. The Home Depot vendors were visible on the builds and in the press, and they were very active with employees to reinforce the great mission of Habitat for Humanity.

  This was even further exemplified at all of the national home building shows throughout the United States. Home Depot certainly learned a great deal from their CRM endeavor with Habitat for Humanity. In fact, they have created another partnership with Kaboom. This partnership has created or refurbished playgrounds in local communities as a result of a major infusion of capital from The Home Depot.

These trends have created even more outlets for companies and corporations to become involved in CRM, and have often proved to be successful for both parties involved in the partnership. Regionalizing, internationalizing, and leveraging with existing partners can reach wide audiences, as well as assist in targeting specific markets or populations.

Targeting Specific Populations

Toward that end, companies must consider their audiences' specific interests and needs. Past trend reports have cited American priorities as public education, crime, and the quality of the environment. Some of the hot issues in 2005 and 2006 continue to be education, affordable housing—especially due to the devastating effects of hurricanes such as Katrina and Rita—immunization, global AIDS, and breast cancer research.

The focus of CRM research continues to be mindful of populations that need help. Consumers worldwide are responding in record numbers to products that pay attention to causes. Companies have begun to pay particularly close attention to the demographic and psychographic profiles, as well as the lifetime value of their customers.

For instance, the Sharper Image gives a certain percentage of all of the proceeds from their air purifiers sold as a licensing fee to the Asthma and Allergy Foundation of America. Samsung supports four causes in its Four Seasons of Hope program, which is comprised of the Joe Torre Safe-At-Home program, the Arnold Palmer Hospital for Children and Women, the Boomer Esiason Foundation, and the Magic Johnson Foundation.

While many successful partnerships have already been created in the CRM field, there remain great opportunities to forge new relationships that can improve brand image and corporate status, and more importantly can enhance the lives of members of the global community. If one follows the components of the win-win philosophies while focusing on the needs of the company and the benefits of CRM, the end results of new and renewed partnerships are limitless.

CHAPTER 4

EXPANDING THE BANDWIDTH OF CAUSE-RELATED MARKETING AND DIVERSITY[1]

Multicultural marketing is a major component of the CRM mix. Leading marketers are now realizing that they can have additional reach and revenue by adding a spin to their campaign. For instance, PepsiCo achieved mammoth leaps of their Smart Spot brands by adding the National Council of La Raza and the National Urban League to their strategic outreach and visibility of the Smart Spot brands.

Pharmaceutical companies have realized that diversity markets through health agencies, such as the American Heart Association and American Diabetes Association, can help achieve their numbers. GlaxoSmithKlein and AstraZeneca have been successful in creating cause-related alliances using the magic of CRM to reach diversity groups. They also use celebrities that appeal to these audiences.

Considering that $500 billion will be spent by gay and lesbian groups globally in 2006, a large sign in Unilever's U.S. headquarters cafeteria reminds their brand managers about this. Diversity groups and their programs and efforts, are continually expanding. Here are the statistics and programs:

Snapshot of the Diversity Market
The Diversity Market 2004
 African American: 12.2%
 Hispanic/Latino: 14.2%
 Asian American: 4.2%
 Native American: 0.8%
 Source: U.S. Census Bureau, 2004 American Community Survey

---

[1]All mission statements and program descriptions come from the home pages of the companies and organizations cited.

Spending Power 2004
African American: 723.1 bil
Hispanic/Latino: 686.3 bil
Asian American: 363.2 bil
Native American: 28.4 bil

Source: Selig Center for Economic Growth, Terry College of Business, University of Georgia 2004

Statistics and Trends

College Education—Bachelor's Degree (numbers in thousands):
Total for population: 35,994
African American: 2,730
Hispanic/Latino: 2,010
Asian American: 2,558

Home Ownership
African American: 51% are householders (13,628/26,665)
Hispanic/Latino: 41% are householders (11,692/28,517)
Asian American: 42% are householders (4,040/9,577)

Number of People per Household
African American: 2.64
Hispanic/Latino: 3.34
Asian American: 2.9

Median Income
African American: 30,134
Hispanic/Latino: 32,241
Asian American: 57,518

Source: U.S. Census Bureau 2004

It is easy to see that individually and collectively, diversity segments of the U.S. population are forming a powerful majority of consumers. This fact is not lost on corporate America. What is lost on much of corporate America is the opportunity to reach these populations by partnering with nonprofit organizations that provide support to them. A wealth of nonprofit sponsorship and partnership opportunities that can help companies targeting major ethnic audiences go unnoticed and untouched by marketers, a baffling circumstance considering the financial strength of diversity audiences and the difficulties many of them face.

Consider the major issues these groups face:

- *The Digital Divide* is a strong enemy of diverse audiences, one that keeps them from entering the new online economy that has mushroomed over the past decade.
- *Access to Quality Healthcare* is among the most disconcerting issues faced by these populations. While medical associations and practitioners have long cried out about the inequality of access, statistics continue to prove an abysmal response by the healthcare system.
- *Financial Empowerment* is one of the most-needed issues to be addressed. By fostering financial literacy and discipline, diversity audiences will be better able to manage their money and grow their individual and collective spending power.
- *Childcare and After-School Programs* have proven to be effective and efficient in helping disadvantaged parents and youth succeed in the American marketplace.
- *Health Conditions*—specifically high blood pressure, diabetes, prostate cancer, and obesity—have particularly high occurrence rates among diversity audiences.

Many NPs have well-developed programs that address these and other issues, which are great ways for a corporation to gain recognition and esteem among members of different diversity markets. Despite the fact that vibrant programs have been developed, a visible leadership role in this area on the corporate level has not been assumed. This makes for an outstanding opportunity for marketers to leverage an extraordinary advantage with the diversity population to capture a largely untapped source of new customers and instill brand loyalty among them.

A review of some large nonprofit diversity initiatives is in order to highlight the opportunities staring marketers in the face and the balance sheet. It is unbelievable that many of these programs and relationship opportunities go untouched by companies that are scrambling for ways to relate to the diverse American population.

Nonprofit Diversity Initiatives

YWCA Branding

In 2004, the YWCA of the USA launched its new branding campaign, "Eliminating Racism, Empowering Women." Here is a bold statement that obviously tells you more than its name; it proclaims its mission statement.

The new brand—supported by a nationwide advertising campaign—introduced the YWCA Hallmark Programs "Racial Justice" and "Women's Economic Advancement." More than 300 YWCA associations nationwide fulfill these initiatives through their community-based programs and services while remaining aligned with YWCA of the USA's overall mission.

Financial empowerment has been a cornerstone of YWCA's rebranding campaign, which has been a major initiative of the organization. Eliminating racism is the main cornerstone of the future for the YWCA. However, with strong mission statements begins the need for programs. Financial empowerment helps the YWCA utilize its chapter network, reinforce branding, and stay focused on its mission.

The empowerment of women, especially financially, is what attracts partners. The program has a rigid curriculum, core values, and an affiliate support system. At the time of this writing, new corporate partnerships are being solidified in the financial services area in order to continue the power of the brand, utilize the vast YWCA network, and deliver both for the new financial partners and the members of the YWCA.

Marketers are beginning to realize that all the diversity audiences combined are beginning to represent the powerful majority of consumers. Here the YWCA has the opportunity to communicate to a specific audience with a powerful distribution of over 2,000 affiliates. Partners such as PepsiCo and Merrill Lynch have exercised the opportunity to do something good and yet increase the power and distribution of their brands.

American Heart Association

The AHA describes its "Search Your Heart Sunday . . . Go Healthy Monday" campaign as "a multi-year, faith-based program created by the American Heart Association to increase heart health and stroke prevention in communities of color." This program was created based on research that showed that African Americans and Latino/Hispanic Americans have a higher risk of death and disability from heart disease and stroke than any other population groups in the United States.

The program entails its religious leaders providing heart health messages to their members during Sunday services and encouraging them to make healthy changes, starting on Mondays and continuing throughout the week. "Search Your Heart" encourages churches to take ownership of the program and make it their own—with materials from the AHA, from the campaign itself, and from program partners.

The AHA has also announced that Health Power, a nonprofit organization actively involved in efforts to improve the health of communities of color, is partnering with the "Search Your Heart" program because of a shared commitment to one goal—to increase heart health and stroke prevention in communities of color.

The challenge of this campaign has been how to reach an audience that needs vital health information. The unique distribution and implementation of this program center on the pastor or minister and his or her appeal to the parishioners. The larger churches have a built-in system for education workshops, training, and distribution. However, unity is difficult, as the penetration varies from church to church.

The growing interest of Americans in losing weight and the higher rate of obesity among African American audiences relative to the general population provides fuel for this targeted program for the American Heart Association. Sponsors have varied in participation as the challenge develops to solidify numbers; however, the AHA has been very diligent in building a powerhouse from a base of support. For instance, in New York, New Jersey, and Connecticut, through the AHA's Heritage Affiliate, GHI Health Insurance has helped with the "Search Your Heart" program not only with funding, but also with credibility and distribution.

American Diabetes Association

As a result of the prevalence of diabetes among diversity populations, the American Diabetes Association (ADA) caters to different diversity segments specifically with their programs. The following are the current diversity programs and initiatives as described by the ADA:

African-American Programs

With the growing trend of new cases of diabetes and pre–diabetes, the ADA is committed to improving the lives of African Americans and their families who are at risk for diabetes.

- *African-American Initiative*
  The ADA has targeted increasing awareness of the seriousness of diabetes and the importance of making healthy lifestyle choices such as moving more and eating healthier.

- *Reach One Teach One: African-American Program*
  The ADA offers a variety of community-based efforts, printed materials, videos, and publications including topics on soul food cooking, getting fit, diabetes 101, and much more.

  African-American churches have always served as the life-center of the community, providing services that nourish the mind, body, and spirit. Given this critical role, the ADA works closely with churches nationwide to promote diabetes education and awareness.

- *Diabetes Day*
  Church pastors across the country spread the gospel of prevention through Diabetes Day. The goals of Diabetes Day are simple: increase awareness about the seriousness of diabetes; increase awareness of risk factors; and inform church members about the resources available through the ADA.

  At a Diabetes Day event, the pastor or a designated appointee shares information with the congregation about the seriousness of diabetes during the service. Out of respect for the religious service, the presentation is very brief (approximately five minutes). All congregation members receive diabetes information. Those at risk for developing the disease are encouraged to get checked for diabetes at their next healthcare visit.

- *Project POWER*
  The American Diabetes Association offers a variety of follow-up activities for churches interested in year-round diabetes

awareness programs such as Project POWER. Project POWER is the Association's program strategy targeting the African American community through the churches. This program was developed to provide churches with a foundation to assist with integrating diabetes awareness messages and healthy living tips into the life of the family and church. These lessons can improve the health of those church members living with diabetes, their families, and even the community.

Project POWER is intended to encourage churches to stay on the battlefield against diabetes, January through December. Project POWER is only available in select markets.

Celebrity sponsors include the Blind Boys of Alabama, Daryl Coley, Ossie Davis, Indianapolis Colts Coach Tony Dungy, performers Marvin Isley and Gladys Knight, Philadelphia Eagles Quarterback Donovan McNabb, Chicago Bears Coach Lovie Smith, and the Dallas Mavericks' Jerry Stackhouse.

Hispanic and Latino Program

Diabetes is an urgent health problem in the Latino community, whose rates of diabetes are double those of non-Latino whites. Getting information to the community about the seriousness of diabetes, its risk factors, and those who may be at risk and ways to help manage the disease is essential. Similar to their African American outreach programs and initiatives, the ADA also caters specifically to the Hispanic and Latino populations. The Diabetes Assistance & Resources program (DAR) is the Latino outreach program of the ADA.

Materials targeting the Hispanic/Latino community, available in English and Spanish, are an integral part of ADA's outreach efforts to help improve the quality of life for Latinos with diabetes. From books to brochures, these publications will give you information on topics ranging from cooking with a Latin flair, to being more physically active, to maintaining a healthy weight.

Community-based activities are another important part of the DAR program. Through fun and informative workshops and activities, community members can learn more about diabetes, the importance of making healthy food choices, and being physically active on a regular basis.

Native American Program

The ADA also created "Awakening the Spirit: Pathways to Diabetes Prevention & Control" to help share important messages about diabetes with the Native American population. Through working with other organizations including the Indian Health Service, developing and disseminating educational materials, and participating in advocacy activities, "Awakening the Spirit" encourages Native Americans to fight diabetes, make healthy food choices, and be more active.

The ADA reports that both nationally and locally, Native American communities around the country are working through "Awakening the Spirit" to encourage Congress to continue funding diabetes education programs in tribal communities. Writing, faxing, calling, and visiting congressional members are several strategies employed at the community level to lobby for issues of concern specifically addressing needs identified by the Native American community.

The National Council of La Raza

The National Council of La Raza (NCLR)—"the largest national Hispanic civil rights and advocacy organization in the United States—works to improve opportunities for Hispanic Americans." NCLR reports that through its network of more than 300 affiliated, community-based organizations, it reaches millions of Hispanics each year in 41 states, Puerto Rico, and the District of Columbia. NCLR conducts applied research, policy analysis, and advocacy, providing a Latino perspective in five key areas: assets/investments, civil rights/immigration, education, employment and economic status, and health. In addition, it provides capacity-building assistance to its affiliates who work at the state and local level to advance opportunities for individuals and families.

NCLR runs several projects geared toward improving and empowering the lives of members of Hispanic and Latino communities. One such project is the Latino Empowerment and Advocacy Project (LEAP), which

> seeks to foster Latino and immigrant civic participation by increasing the engagement of these communities in the political process, focusing on unregistered, newly registered, and infrequent voters, by (1) training a

multi-state network of community-based organizations (CBOs) to orga-
nize field campaigns and promote sustained civic education and partici-
pation; (2) testing and documenting campaign strategies to identify effec-
tive models that reduce participation barriers and increase interest in the
process; (3) conducting research, policy analysis, and advocacy to promote
policies, programs, and investments that support growth in immigrant and
Latino civic participation; and (4) linking this emerging electorate with
nonpartisan, issue-based advocacy campaigns promoting full integration
of immigrants in mainstream society.

Another project is the NCLR Home Ownership Network
(NHN), which is funded by the Department of Housing and Urban
Development (HUD) and the private home-buying industry. NHN
affiliates are incorporated into the network based on an annual appli-
cation process in which target plans are submitted to NCLR for
review based on several criteria, including need for counseling services
in the area and quality of services provided. In return, NHN agencies
become eligible for HUD grants and technical assistance from NCLR.
NHN's core service is pre-purchase homeownership counseling,
which targets first-time homebuyers. Unique to the NHN model is
the emphasis on individual one-on-one counseling, which is critical to
Latino families unfamiliar with mainstream financial services. Group
home-buyer education, post-purchase counseling and education, de-
fault and delinquency counseling, and rental counseling augment the
one-on-one sessions.

La Raza is a particularly notable diversity nonprofit because of the
number of corporate sponsors with whom they work. Senior members of 26 corporations sit on the board, and they have several strategic partnerships and grant programs with prominent companies.
NCLR is involved in a hiring partnership with The Home Depot that
began in 2005, and it has received grant money for the Raza Development Fund from Allstate Insurance (2001) and Chase (2004). Citigroup also launched a strategic partnership with NCLR in 2003.

National Urban League

The National Urban League (NUL) states that its mission is "to enable
African Americans to secure economic self-reliance, parity, power and

civil rights." NUL was established in 1910, and prides itself on being "the nation's oldest and largest community-based movement devoted to empowering African Americans to enter the economic and social mainstream." Today, the NUL, from its headquarters in New York City, spearheads the nonpartisan efforts of its over 100 local affiliates in 35 states and the District of Columbia providing direct services to more than 2 million people nationwide through programs, advocacy, and research.

The NUL also has several different relationships with corporate sponsors and partners. State Farm Insurance partners with the NUL in the form of a three-pronged, three-year initiative. Focusing on education and youth, it is part of the campaign for African American achievement.

Exxon Mobil announced a new collaborative effort to help identify and attract minority dealers and distributors to own and operate Exxon and Mobil service stations in 2005, a project that aligns with a "key objective of the National Urban League . . . to expand economic empowerment," according to NUL president and CEO Marc H. Morial. Heineken USA sponsors the NUL Young Professionals-Heineken USA Rising Star Program, an essay contest that aligns with the NUL's economic empowerment agenda.

Denny's, the nation's largest family restaurant chain, has also partnered with the NUL. Denny's pledged to raise up to $1 million for the Urban League over the course of a year (October 2005 – October 2006). Participating Denny's restaurants donate $.20 cents from the sale of each All-American Slam(R) to support the NUL's education and youth programs. Part of the proceeds will be used to develop a CD-ROM targeting middle and high school students seeking admission to college. Proceeds will also fund after-school and education projects at the NUL's affiliate centers.

Magic Johnson Foundation

The Magic Johnson Foundation was founded in December 1991 by Earvin "Magic" Johnson "to identify and support community-based organizations that address the educational, health, and social needs of children, young adults and inner-city communities throughout the nation." The foundation donates needed funds to organizations that provide HIV/AIDS prevention and healthcare education to the minority community.

It is the only foundation to successfully address the digital divide among minorities on a nationwide level. In fact, the foundation opens technology centers in underserved communities with excellent programs that provide children the necessary computer training to learn and compete in the information age.

The Magic Johnson Foundation views technology and web-based learning as the most effective and comprehensive method to accomplish its goals of closing the gap in the digital divide and transitioning residents from financial dependence to financial independence.

Each technology center will provide a customized curriculum in a noncompetitive, structured environment that will provide education on numerous topics ranging from introduction to computers to Cisco certifications. Program participation is free to community residents.

Magic Johnson also lent his name and presence to the MCI History Makers event. The History Makers represents the single largest archival project of its kind in the world. Not since the recording of former slaves during the federal Work Projects Administration (WPA) movement of the 1930s has there been a systematic and wide-scale attempt to capture and preserve the testimonies of African Americans. Local students and teachers gathered for the launch of a historical treasure at "Meet the History Makers: A Day of Education" at Los Angeles's California African American Museum. Magic Johnson's involvement not only benefited the event, but also built a connection between Magic and MCI.

Human Rights Campaign

The Human Rights Campaign (HRC) is "the largest national gay, lesbian, bisexual and transgender advocacy organization that envisions an America where GLBT people are ensured of their basic equal rights, and can be open, honest and safe at home, at work and in the community." HRC has close to 600,000 members, all committed to making this vision of equality a reality.

Founded in 1980, HRC effectively lobbies Congress, provides campaign support to fair-minded candidates, and works to educate the public on a wide array of topics affecting GLBT Americans, including relationship recognition, workplace, family, and health issues. The HRC Foundation—an HRC-affiliated organization—engages in research and provides public education and programming.

There have been vast and varied sponsors of many HRC Foundation programs to date, some highlights of which include

- Volvo Cars of North America, LLC: For any new purchase or lease between January 1, 2005 to December 31, 2005, Volvo donated $500 to HRC.
- When HRC members, their families, and their friends come to Chase for home financing needs, Chase will give a $350 rebate off closing costs.
- In addition to supporting the activities of HRC both financially and through volunteer involvements, Prudential has established a special discount on its long-term care products available to all HRC members.
- When making a reservation on American Airlines's AA.com or elsewhere, all you need to do is provide them with HRC's Business ExtrAA account number and HRC earns valuable points. This can be done in addition to using your personal American AAdvantage number.
- Washington Mutual is offering HRC members special savings on home purchase or refinance.
- Nike, a global company, acts as a sponsor for HRC, stating, "The Gay Lesbian Bisexual Transgender and Friends Network aims to increase awareness and understanding of Nike's GLBT community through educational and supportive events, and demonstrates Nike's commitment to diversity through outreach to the local, national and global GLBT community."
- Support Equality & Awareness @ Shell Oil
  "The mission of SEA Shell is to provide support for members and co-workers and to promote equality for employees regardless of sexual orientation or gender identification. We will create awareness in management of issues and concerns affecting people in a diverse workplace, and community inclusive of sexual orientation and gender identification."

In addition to the organizations and programs described thus far, there are other events that make diversity communities a notable presence in society, and also provide an opportunity to become involved in different diversity communities.

Million Man March

The Million Man March was an African American march of protest and unity convened by Nation of Islam leader Louis Farrakhan in Washington, D.C. on October 16, 1995. The actual number of participants is disputed by critics. The event included efforts to register African Americans to vote in U.S. elections and increase black involvement in volunteerism and community activism. Speakers also offered a strong criticism of the conservative offensive of Republicans after the 1994 congressional elections (most notably the Contract with America), characterized as an attack on programs like welfare, Medicaid, housing programs, student aid programs, and education programs.

The Million Man March draws specific attention to the issues of one specific diversity population, and can also generate specific celebrity and press interest. For instance, on Sunday July 24, 2005, Kanye West was presented with the 2005 Million Man March Image Award on behalf of the Board of Directors of Million Man March 10 Anniversary, The Millions More Movement.

Effects of 2005 Hurricane Season

While some events are planned to draw attention to certain diversity populations and communities, other events occur unexpectedly and force us to give them attention. Examples of this are the natural disasters that struck the US Gulf Coast. Hurricanes Katrina and Rita struck neighborhoods that were comprised of many members of diversity populations.

Snapshot of Hurricane Effects and Recovery Effort[2]:

Estimated Cost	The American Red Cross estimates that Hurricane Katrina relief efforts will exceed $2 billion, meeting the urgent needs of Hurricane Katrina and Rita survivors in a number of areas—including food and shelter, emergency financial assistance, and physical and mental health services.

---

[2]Estimations based on information provided on the Red Cross homepage (http://www.redcross.org).

Financial Assistance	Red Cross financial assistance is provided in a variety of ways, including client assistance cards, vouchers, checks, and cash. The Red Cross estimates it will distribute financial assistance to approximately 1.2 million families (more than 3.7 million hurricane survivors).
Shelters/Temporary Housing	Since Hurricane Katrina made landfall, the Red Cross has provided hurricane survivors with nearly 3.41 million overnight stays in nearly 1,100 shelters across 27 states and the District of Columbia.
Relief Workers	More than 213,630 Red Cross disaster relief workers from all 50 states, Puerto Rico, and the Virgin Islands have responded to their neighbors in need.
Feeding Operations	The Red Cross, in coordination with the Southern Baptist Convention, has served more than 26.7 million hot meals and 23.8 million snacks to hurricane survivors to date.

The American Red Cross is one of the most extensive and diversity-conscious organizations in its relief efforts. Providing relief, including vouchers, vital food assistance, and housing support, has been a cornerstone of the American Red Cross. Katrina, Rita, and other global disasters demonstrate the work of the American Red Cross and the Federation of the Red Crescent societies in action.

Corporate citizens like Lowe's, Microsoft, and others have also been extremely helpful in ensuring diverse audiences survive. The program "Your Help Counts" demonstrates a retail initiative where consumers can give $1, $2, or $5 to support those most in need.

Existing Corporate Programs

Some corporations have begun their own diversity initiatives without an event or occurrence to spur action.

ABC Radio

The federal government and healthcare communities were looking for effective and creative ways to inform, motivate, and empower African Americans to improve their health, and to involve the private sector in this process. The Department of Health and Human Services' (DHHS) "Initiative to Eliminate Racial and Ethnic Disparities in Health" identified a "health gap" between African American communities that needed to be closed. Wishing to give something back to its millions of African American listeners, in 2001, urban media leader ABC Radio launched "Closing the Health Gap," an awareness campaign for the African American community on the significance of being healthy. It aimed to motivate a change in behavior among African Americans that would help close the health gap. Partnerships between ABC Radio Networks and National Advertisers were formed to assist in generating information and momentum for this awareness campaign. ABC Radio Networks also partnered with the DHHS in this endeavor.

Lifetime

Lifetime cable network's sweeping "Our Lifetime Commitment" public outreach campaigns aim to make a positive difference in the lives of women and girls, as well as their families, through education, awareness, and legislation. The campaigns leverage the network's multimedia capabilities and reach to include original television programming, PSAs, online content, community outreach, advocacy for national legislation, fundraising events, and newsletters.

"Our Lifetime Commitment" serves as the brand encompassing several outreach campaigns, including

- *"Stop Violence Against Women"*
  Lifetime has joined with more than 70 organizations including V-Day and the YWCA of the USA in myriad activities to stop violence against women and girls. The network's advocacy efforts include shining the spotlight on its partner organizations and offering a page on its website as a valuable resource for information and help.

- *"Every Woman Counts"*
  Lifetime's public education campaign "to empower women of all ages and diverse backgrounds to become part of the democratic process as voters and future candidates," "Every Woman Counts," has partnered with 15 women's voting organizations including the National Organization for Women. In 2004, the network launched a series of public service announcements encouraging women to vote. Currently, the program serves as an information center on political issues, women in politics, and relevant articles, and conducts polls on voter issues.

- *"Be Your Own Hero"*
  Lifetime's "campaign to raise confidence in girls and women by celebrating their strengths, talents and determination" targets community outreach programs with a collective of partnering nonprofits including the YWCA of the USA and the White House Project.

- *"Caring for Kids"*
  This campaign promotes quality early-childhood education and childcare. Program partners include more than 30 leading advocates for children and early education such as YWCA of the USA, Salvation Army, Child Care Aware, and Girl Scouts of the U.S.A. For this effort, Lifetime produced a PSA, "Resume," which conveyed the need for quality early-childhood education and its positive influence on the well-being of children.

While many of the aforementioned nonprofit and corporate programs have attained some level of respect and success, it is always essential to remain sensitive to diversity audiences. One example of the danger of insensitivity to diversity audiences occurred with the Masters Golf Tournament.

The Masters Golf Tournament is considered the most popular event in all of golf. Held annually at the Augusta National Golf Club in Augusta, Georgia, the tournament has been sold out for almost 30 years. Members of the Augusta National Golf Club, owner and host of the Tournament, include 300 of the world's most powerful and wealthy businessmen and politicians, including former General Electric CEO Jack Welch, former Secretary of State George Shultz, and Arnold Palmer. The event also draws major sponsorships from the highest echelons of corporate America.

In 2003, after discovering that the Augusta National Golf Club did not grant membership to women, Martha Burk, chair of the National Council of Women's Organizations (NCWO), contacted the club's president, William "Hooter" Johnson, and challenged him to revamp their membership policies to include women. (The first African American member was admitted to the invitation-only club in 1990.)

Johnson rebuked Burk's efforts in a response letter, and took the offensive by crafting and disseminating a press release chiding Burk for her "clearly coercive" tactics. The press release cemented Johnson's stance that he "will not make additional comments or respond to the taunts and gripes artificially generated by the corporate campaign." Burk retaliated by taking on the tournament's corporate sponsors and urging them to suspend sponsorship of the tournament.

Burk's efforts proved to be successful and far-reaching: The 2003 tournament lost some $20 million worth of sponsors because of the discrimination claim, a move made by Johnson to shield his partner corporations from fallout caused by the dispute.

Major corporations that revoked entirely their sponsorships or reduced their participation included Citigroup, Coca-Cola, IBM, General Motors, Cadillac, Georgia Pacific, Southern Company, JP Morgan Chase Lucent Technologies, and American Express.

One of the world's prime sports advertising properties, the Masters gets the highest television ratings among golf tournaments. Without Citigroup, Coca-Cola, and IBM on board as the tournament's telecast sponsors, the Augusta National Golf Club ended up financing the major sporting event from its own coffers. As a result, in 2003 and again in 2004, the Masters were viewed by more than 13 million viewers without commercials (on national broadcasts).

Clearly, there are many ways for corporations and brands to reach and influence purchase decision among the new majority in America, including the boycotting of public entities that are insensitive to ethnic and racial issues. The shifting of the marketing landscape becomes particularly important as sponsorship revenues are slowly being tied to social and multicultural issues. Hopefully, the shift will gain speed and reach critical mass within a short time.

One of the driving forces in the shift is the power of women, illustrated by the 88 million women that watch Lifetime Television each week. This is another group that can be thought of as a diversity audience historically held back from career success. However, many women who have broken through the glass ceiling—particularly Carole Black and her team of senior executives at Lifetime Television, Meredith Wagner, Mary Dixon, and Geralyn Lucas—have brought to light issues that affect their group and have helped the brand soar to new heights by creating a legacy of corporate social responsibility for the network.

As traditionally marginalized groups reach positions of influence in their companies, they might follow the example of Carole Black and her executive team by making support of diversity issues a cornerstone of their marketing platforms. They need to shrug off the notion that they may be seen as kowtowing to pressure, and look ahead with the knowledge that supporting large audiences is simply good business.

PART II

CAUSE MARKETING REVIEW

CHAPTER 5

RETAIL CASE STUDY

The Challenge and the Strategy

The U.S. retail market earns hundreds of billions of dollars annually and stands at the forefront of high-profile, high-impact cause marketing efforts. Wal-Mart and SUBWAY are considered two of today's biggest retail powerhouses. It is only natural that two companies with such financial clout would want to be involved in philanthropic endeavors. Wal-Mart and SUBWAY are just two of the retail leaders that have effected positive change by raising billions of dollars for their nonprofit partners. So why should retailers join in CRM efforts? Simple: By aligning themselves with charitable organizations, they automatically improve their corporate image and significantly increase reach and revenue among their target demographics. The benefit these retailers receive from joining in cause-related efforts has no bounds. These efforts elevate the retailer's image and leverage traffic to support the initiative. Following is an in-depth look at these two cause marketing partnerships that have had a significant global impact: Wal-Mart and SUBWAY.

Wal-Mart

In the 1980s, Wal-Mart became one of the most successful retailers in America. Sales grew to $26 billion by 1989, compared to $1 billion in 1980. At the end of the 1980s, there were nearly 1,400 stores in the U.S. Because of their tremendous success, Wal-Mart Stores, Inc. branched out into warehouse clubs with the first SAM'S CLUB in 1983. This supercenter featured a complete grocery department along with 36 departments of general merchandise. Wal-Mart was creating a solid reputation as a company that refused to compromise on its unrivaled customer service, regardless of its rapid growth in annual sales.

Wal-Mart is famous not only for its span of merchandise and low prices, but also for the helpful attitude of its employees. Now as the world's number-one retailer, with more than 5,700 stores—including some 1,350 discount stores, nearly 2,000 combination discount and grocery stores, and 550 warehouse stores (SAM'S CLUB)—Wal-Mart is looking to expand in Central and Eastern Europe (particularly Hungary and Poland) and is exploring possibilities in India. Because of these reasons, it is no wonder Wal-Mart has chosen to delve into the field of cause marketing.

The Wal-Mart store, SAM'S CLUB, and their distribution centers established a charitable foundation as a way of responding to the needs of their local communities. In 2005 alone, Wal-Mart donated more than $200 million to help charities and organizations throughout the U.S. This foundation is based on the philosophy of "operating globally and giving back locally" and focuses specifically on education, children, and local communities. For example, the typical supercenter raises or gives $30,000 to $50,000 a year to local charitable needs ranging from youth programs to literacy councils.

Wal-Mart's approach to community involvement combines both financial and volunteer support. The company encourages its employees to be as involved in their local communities as possible. Wal-Mart's charitable giving has garnered positive recognition for the company. *Forbes* magazine recognized Wal-Mart in 2002 as one of the most philanthropic companies in America. Also in 2002, Wal-Mart was presented with the Ron Brown Award for Corporate Leadership, a presidential award that recognizes companies for outstanding achievement in employee and community relations. In 2003 and 2004, Wal-Mart was named by *Fortune* magazine as the most admired company in the United States. In 2004, the National Committee for Employer Support of the Guard and Reserve, in conjunction with the Secretary of Defense, honored Wal-Mart as a 2004 Secretary of Defense Employer Support Freedom Award recipient.

As we can see, Wal-Mart supports programs that focus on positive change. The company sponsors many organizations, including the American Red Cross, Community Matching Grants, United Way, the National Center for Missing and Exploited Children, and the Salvation Army. Wal-Mart has focused particularly on youth programs, and one of its most significant relationships is with the Children's Miracle Network.

The Children's Miracle Network

In 1988, Wal-Mart became a corporate sponsor of the Children's Miracle Network (CMN), a nonprofit organization dedicated to saving and improving the lives of children by raising funds for children's hospitals across North America. CMN is also one of the world's leading children's charities. This alliance of 170 premier hospitals for kids around the country is dedicated to raising money for children with cancer, pediatric AIDS, muscular dystrophy, heart disease, leukemia, sickle cell anemia, asthma, and accident trauma. CMN hospitals have pioneered many breakthroughs in pediatric medicine including cancer treatments, brain surgery, prosthetics, and organ transplant techniques. Each year, these hospitals provide more than $2.5 billion in charitable care.

CMN raises funds through a number of corporate sponsors and events such as the annual Children's Miracle Network Celebration broadcast. Since 1983, CMN has raised more than $2.2 billion for hospitalized children—most of which is donated a dollar or two at a time by individuals throughout the United States and Canada.

How and Why the Relationship Works

As a corporate sponsor for CMN, Wal-Mart (and its associates) sell paper "Miracle Balloons" at $1 each, positioned at registers in 3,700 participating Wal-Mart stores and SAM'S CLUB locations, neighborhood markets, and distribution centers. Other efforts to raise money for CMN include bake sales, softball and golf tournaments, fashion shows, and other activities during "Miracle Months." These activities help fund new medical services, as well as life-saving research into childhood diseases such as pediatric cancer, cystic fibrosis, and pediatric AIDS.

Here are some other specific examples from the Wal-Mart website of new hospital services that Wal-Mart raised through fundraising in 2005:

- A newborn intensive care unit ambulance to transport critically ill children to Children's Medical Center in Dallas, Texas.
- A Wal-Mart safety corner, where children are educated on the importance of safety at Children's Memorial Hospital in Chicago, IL.

- The "Angel One" helicopter used to transport seriously ill patients from rural areas to Arkansas Children's Hospital in Little Rock.
- A neonatal intensive care unit for the Medical university of South Carolina Children's Hospital in Charleston.
- A traveling asthma clinic, the Breathmobile, to assist children at the Children's Hospital in Phoenix.

By tapping into its customer base at the point of purchase, in 2005 at the start of its annual "Miracle Months" fundraising efforts from April through June, CMN announced that Wal-Mart has raised and donated more than $300 million for CMN over its 18-year sponsorship period. Over 1 million Wal-Mart associates help 17 million children a year. In 2004 alone, Wal-Mart Stores, Inc. associates raised more than $31 million for CMN.

SUBWAY

SUBWAY® entered its 39th year of operation in 2004 as the world's largest submarine sandwich chain. With over 25,000 restaurants in 75 countries, SUBWAY has become one of the principal players in the fast-food industry. The franchisors of SUBWAY restaurants employ more than 150,000 men and women throughout the system worldwide. As of 2003 their total sales were at $6.8 billion, which is no surprise considering the chain serves approximately 1,900 sandwiches every 60 seconds all over the world. Although SUBWAY may compete with fast-food companies like Burger King, McDonald's, and Taco Bell, it is certainly in a class all its own. Unlike most of its competitors, SUBWAY's target marketing goal focuses on healthy eating habits and overall well-being, yet still offers the elements of freshness and taste. SUBWAY's direct marketing reaches to consumers 18–49 who lead active lifestyles, and who are seeking nutrition as well as taste. There are nearly 2 million different sandwich combinations available on the SUBWAY menu, so lack of variety is never an issue.

To prove their new, healthier direction, in 2000 SUBWAY began using Jared Fogle as their spokesperson. Jared is the young man who lost 245 lbs. by eating nothing but SUBWAY sandwiches for almost a year in a diet program he created himself. Jared ate a six-inch SUBWAY turkey sub for lunch and a foot-long SUBWAY Veggie Delite sub for dinner. He stayed away from any non-diet beverages, and occasionally he would eat a bag of baked chips. Jared also included lots of walking as part of his program, which helped him lose 245 lbs. in a little less than a year. Because of Jared's appearance in a series of SUBWAY television commercials, he inspired many other overweight individuals to choose healthier options, like some of the SUBWAY subs. This was a great marketing hook for SUBWAY, inspiring them to sponsor the American Heart Association in 2002, to further increase their health credibility.

Most recently, SUBWAY created the Fresh Steps program to complement their message of healthy eating and lifestyle. This initiative was inspired by the thousands of letters the company receives from kids and adults describing their goal to improve their quality of life and make healthier choices. It also made people aware of SUBWAY relationship with the American Heart Association and the important information AHA offers on health.

The American Heart Association

A revolutionary group of physicians and social workers formed the first Association for the Prevention and Relief of Heart Disease in New York City in 1915. There was a significant lack of information on heart disease at that time, and most patients were told only to get bed rest. Eventually this organization became the American Heart Association. Today, because of medical care, extensive research, and an organization like the AHA, there is credible heart disease and stroke information available to everyone as well as more effective treatment and prevention.

During the 1990s, the AHA came across significant scientific research on heart disease and began to shift its focus from laboratories and clinics to physicians' offices and American households. The AHA took positions on important issues and made clear, simple statements about controlling risk factors so the information was more accessible and comprehendible for the general public—not just physicians and scientists. Through staff and volunteers, a strategy was developed for improving affiliate research programs and a new division that dealt with stroke and emergency cardiac care was created.

The AHA was very opposed to the tobacco industry and had no problem stating this publicly, as tobacco smoking can be a cause of heart disease. Despite opposition from tobacco companies, the AHA continued to advocate nonsmoking to the general public, especially focusing on youth.

Today the AHA is considered a national voluntary health agency whose mission is to reduce disability and death from cardiovascular diseases and stroke. The organization has also set a lofty goal, calling for the reduction of coronary heart disease, stroke, and risk by 25 percent by 2010.

How and Why the Relationship Works

Because SUBWAY brand strongly believes that better health leads to a higher quality of life, the company chose to sponsor the AHA.

SUBWAY has a large number of customers who have serious problems managing their food balance. Although they do have many healthy choices, many of these customers are not particularly healthy. Generally, SUBWAY customers are people on the go or who don't have the time to really think about what goes into the preparation of a meal. A customer may grab a meatball sub as opposed to a healthier choice. But SUBWAY created "7 under 6" sandwiches, offering seven subs that are under six grams of fat (now they offer eight such subs).

For the AHA, partnering with SUBWAY was a natural fit. SUBWAY is able to reach consumers that the AHA couldn't necessarily access. Frequently, the more educated the consumers, the more sophisticated their food choice. Those who do not understand the principles of healthy eating often have the wrong impression of what is beneficial to health and what is not. For the AHA, joining SUBWAY was a wonderful opportunity to meet a whole range of new influencers, for example, moms on the go who influence their families, busy kids who need healthy snacks or healthy lunches, and 9-to-5 workers with limited lunch time. SUBWAY also incorporated helpful nutritional information about their menu on napkins, tray liners, and cups. The company has tagged the American Heart symbol on all of their TV announcements so that consumers are able to start focusing on the two in a fun and simple way.

SUBWAY is a big sponsor of events for the AHA. As an addition to the Fresh Steps program, the company supports the AHA's "Jump

Rope for Heart" childhood physical activity and nutrition program. This school-site program, celebrating its 25th anniversary, reaches more than 4 million kids annually with positive messages about heart-healthy lifestyles.

Not only is SUBWAY concerned with childhood obesity, it also nationally sponsors the AHA's Heart Walk. The Heart Walk is an annual 5K walk with a goal to be a fun, healthy activity where the whole family can participate. Spanning 750 cities across America, the American Heart Walk is now in its ninth year and is the AHA's premier fundraiser. Included in the Heart Walk are nationwide event fundraisers to help fight heart disease and stroke—the number one and three most common reasons for deaths in the country. Since their inception, these walks have raised over $216 million to improve the quality of life.

Mini Case Studies

Here is a brief look into some other retail/nonprofit relationships:

The Home Depot and KaBOOM!

In the mid-'90s, The Home Depot—the world's largest home improvement specialty retailer—joined forces with KaBOOM!, a national NP that works with its corporate partners to help improve communities by building and renovating playgrounds and skate parks in "children-rich and playground-poor markets" across the country.

The retailer awards community grants, funds surveys, and sponsors high-profile initiatives such as KaBOOM!'s "Racing to Play," a campaign in which NASCAR champ Tony Stewart and other Joe Gibbs racing drivers and crew members join with volunteers and local Home Depot stores to build racing-themed playgrounds in one day just prior to a weekend NASCAR race.

In almost a decade of sponsorship, The Home Depot has provided millions of dollars in financial support, high-quality building materials, and the volunteer efforts of more than 40,000 Team Depot associates, who join with community residents to build safe places for kids to play. By the end of 2005, the company estimates that it will have built and funded approximately 400 KaBOOM! playground projects.

In July 2005, The Home Depot and KaBOOM! announced an unprecedented community initiative to create and refurbish "1,000 playspaces in 1,000 days" throughout North America. As part of the three-year program, the retailer "will invest $25 million and nearly one million volunteer hours in support of this program, which is expected to benefit 1.5 million parents and children."

Darell Hammond, co-founder and CEO of KaBOOM!, says the partnership with The Home Depot has also created a snowball effect of support for the nonprofit. In an interview with *Cause Marketing Forum*, Hammond explains:

> *Thanks to that partnership, we probably have 85% name recognition among building supply companies that sell to The Home Depot. Those firms see us as a viable vehicle for creating programs that will lead to incremental sales at The Home Depot. Stanley Tools, for example, recently gave us a $250,000 donation as part of a program that was featured on the cover of The Home Depot catalog and that received end-aisle displays in Home Depot stores. (http://www.causemarketingforum.org/page2. asp?ID=232)*

Lowe's and Habitat for Humanity International

Lowe's, the world's second-largest home improvement retailer, leverages its resources and reach to support nonprofits such as Habitat for Humanity International.

The global NP is an ecumenical Christian housing ministry that builds and rehabilitates houses through the donations of money and materials, as well as with the help of volunteer labor and homeowner (partner) families. (Habitat houses are sold to partner families at no profit and financed with no-interest loans.)

As national underwriter for Habitat, Lowe's addresses the nationwide issue of substandard housing by sponsoring outreach campaigns such as Women Build, in which diverse groups of women help build homes for families in need. Support from the retailer has resulted in at least 150 new Women Build homes in cities across America in 2005 alone.

Lowe's also serves as a sponsor of Habitat's annual Jimmy Carter Work Project. Each year, former U.S. President Jimmy Carter and his wife Rosalynn—who have been involved with Habitat since 1984—give a week of their time and effort to build homes and raise awareness for the need of affordable housing. The Jimmy Carter Work Project takes place at a different location each year and draws volunteers from around the world.

In 2005, Lowe's announced that it had committed $10 million to Habitat programs over the following five years.

Target and Education

Target's commitment "to support and empower the communities its stores serve" is realized in the retailer's giving back of more than $2 million each week to programs, schools, and neighborhoods across the United States. Target offers store-based grants that support projects promoting childhood education, the arts, and family violence prevention. Several of Target's education-based initiatives include

- "Take Charge of Education," a program that has allowed the retailer to donate more than $154 million through fundraising dollars since the campaign's April 1997 launch. Through this program, Target donates an amount equal to 1 percent of Target Visa and Target Card purchases made at Target and Target.com, and 1/2 percent of Target Visa purchases made elsewhere, to the eligible K–12 school of a customer's choice. More than nine million Target cardholders and 106,000 schools participate in the program each year.
- Funding for reading and art appreciation via grants for arts and cultural experiences as well as reading grants that award funds to schools, libraries, and nonprofits that promote reading.
- "All-Around Scholarships," volunteer-based college scholarships that reward students for volunteer work as well as academic achievement.
- "Start Something," a "dream-building" program (inspired by Tiger and Earl Woods's book *Start Something*) that helps children identify and achieve their dreams and goals. Following the program, participants are awarded $5,000 in grant funds.

Additionally, Target Volunteers offer free help for schools across the nation, and Target offers real estate on its website, Target.com, as an online resource for parents and teachers.

IKEA and UNICEF

UNICEF actively encourages the welfare of youth and over the years has joined forces with multinational corporations in order to achieve the largest support base possible. This allows UNICEF to find the mutual benefits for themselves as well as their corporate sponsors. Because of their many pioneering partnerships, UNICEF has created "global cause-related marketing strategies, creative employee programs, and vital emergency-relief appeals tailored for global corporations." UNICEF's global partnerships are built not only to meet UNICEF's primary objectives and marketing initiatives, but also to focus on the partners.

IKEA, a manufacturer and retailer of home furnishings worldwide, is highly committed to corporate social responsibility. Because of this, it was natural for them to support UNICEF programs. For over 10 years, IKEA has supported UNICEF through CRM promotions and donations on a national level. In the United States, IKEA is an essential component of the U.S. Fund for UNICEF's outreach, bringing in sales of UNICEF greeting cards, the national Trick-or-Treat for UNICEF program, and most recently a new CRM initiative called the BRUM stuffed teddy bear, created in 2003. Two dollars from the sale of every bear (which retails for $6.99) were donated to support UNICEF's programs for children affected by war.

In August 2000, IKEA joined forced with UNICEF and initiated a child-rights program that focused on the prevention and elimination of child labor in 200 villages across Northern India. After the Asian tsunami of 2004, IKEA stores worldwide banded together to support UNICEF relief efforts in the devastated areas. IKEA supports UNICEF programs through in-kind assistance, as well as contributing on global and national levels. IKEA has donated thousands of blankets and sheets to Indonesian tsunami victims, as well as those in Sri Lanka. Because of their shared commitment to social responsibility, IKEA and UNICEF's partnership continues to harvest mutual benefits, and their partnership is certain to grow.

Kmart and the March of Dimes

Founded in 1938, the nonprofit March of Dimes was created to improve the health of babies by preventing birth defects, infant mortality rates, and most recently to find out more about the causes of premature pregnancy. Over the years, March of Dimes has funded research programs, community service ventures, educational courses, and sponsorship to save babies.

For 13 consecutive years, Kmart Corporation has partnered with the March of Dimes. As a national corporate partner, Kmart and its associates, along with their customers, have raised nearly $43 million for the nonprofit. This is the largest single donation by any corporation in the history of the organization, proving to be one of the most successful philanthropic initiatives of its kind.

Kmart created an in-store promotion selling paper sneakers to represent the WalkAmerica campaign. Kmart customers have purchased more than 4.5 million paper sneakers for one dollar each. All of these proceeds go to the local communities in which they are purchased. Kmart gathers employees, friends, and families to join in WalkAmerica to support March of Dimes and their important cause. In 2004, the company contributed over $4.9 million to March of Dimes through WalkAmerica, representing a 30 percent increase over 2003.

CHAPTER 6

AMERICA ON THE MOVE AND PEPSICO CASE STUDY

The Challenge and the Strategy

It has been widely claimed that the United States is the most over-weight country in the world. According to the America on the Move (AOM) Foundation, more than 60 percent of American adults do not exercise at the federally recommended amount of 30 minutes daily, and 25 percent of American adults do not exercise at all. According to a recent Harris Poll survey conducted by AOM (http://www.americaonthemove.org) Americans spend 7.7 hours per day sitting and four hours per day watching television and play-ing computer games. More than 120 million Americans, or 64.5 per-cent of the adult population, are overweight, and almost 59 million, or 31 percent, are obese. As a result, the incidence of more than 30 weight-related preventable illnesses has increased, driving up health-care costs (America spends $117 billion a year on these diseases) and reducing workplace productivity.

The challenge: to help Americans make positive changes to improve health and stem the tide of obesity and weight-related preventable illnesses in the United States. The strategy: to create awareness and motivate people into action.

The America on the Move Foundation

The bones of the AOM Foundation were built in 1998 as the out-growth of a 200-person conference on fat-modified foods in the diet. The group—which included James O. Hill, Ph.D., director of the Center for Human Nutrition at the University of Colorado Health Sciences Center; and John C. Peters, Ph.D., associate director of Procter & Gamble's Nutrition Science Institute—came to the consen-sus that primary focus should be placed on evolving the American lifestyle.

A fraction of the conference attendees gathered to develop this concept and focused on doing so via private-public partnership. Their aim was to design a consumer-based partnership whose initiatives targeted the consumer and expanded to the community. The partnership could subsequently garner media coverage and influence, ultimately affecting the American lifestyle for the better.

With this framework in mind, Dr. Peters and Dr. Hill established the Partnership to Promote Healthy Eating and Active Living (PPHEAL) in 1999. Its mission: "To promote healthy eating and physical activity lifestyle behaviors through a public/private partnership grounded on consumer understanding."

Research conducted by the nonprofit demonstrated that "most Americans can stop weight gain by making simple changes each day. Walking an extra 2,000 steps each day, and eating 100 fewer calories each day is enough for most Americans to create a balance between energy expenditure and calorie consumption and sufficient to stop the current average rate of weight gain of one to two pounds per year" (*Science*, Feb. 7, 2003).

Turning science into action, Peters and Hill developed a plan designed to inspire Americans "to engage in fun, simple ways to become more active, eat more healthfully and, as a result achieve and maintain a healthy weight." They selected Colorado—one of the healthiest states in the country—to launch their pilot initiative. "Colorado on the Move" proved to be a success at getting people started on making small changes toward a healthier lifestyle. Peters deemed their program "the on-ramp to wellness."

As their efforts gained traction, the pair worked on expanding their pilot initiative, spending two years developing a national initiative while delaying discussions with other public health organizations that approached the nonprofit about getting involved.

In March 2003, PPHEAL launched America on the Move. Their objectives: to inspire Americans to engage in fun, simple ways to become more active, eat more healthfully, and, as a result, achieve and maintain a healthy weight; to create a grassroots network of state affiliates to build health-promoting communities that support and inspire individual behavior and community changes; to manage a strong AOM national research network, comprised of its academic partners, its public-private board of directors, and other researchers leading the nation in healthy living; and to encourage public and private partnerships at the national, state, and local levels to build the capacity, reach, and support needed for individual and community behavior change.

For an evolution of the American lifestyle to work, Peters believes, the private corporation has an important part to play. "Since they are seen as part of the problem, they should be a part of the solution," he says.

AOM's next step: partnering with a corporate sponsor. According to Laura Simonds, AOM's executive director, AOM seeks sponsors who are looking to increase awareness of AOM's message and help promote it, and who are committed to a business strategy of healthful living—both internally and externally.

As the AOM team sought out corporations that create and promote healthier options for eating and living, PepsiCo—which was developing its first health and wellness program—was looking for the right NP to get behind.

PepsiCo

Responding to consumers' increased awareness and concern about their dietary intake (and that of their families), PepsiCo created the Smart Spot™ line of products to provide a wide array of better product choices for consumers.

PepsiCo's Smart Spot products meet nutrition criteria established by the Food and Drug Administration and the National Academy of Sciences. The products must contain at least 10 percent of the daily value of a targeted nutrient (i.e., protein, fiber, calcium, iron, vitamin A, vitamin C) and meet limits for fat, saturated fat, trans fat, cholesterol, sodium, and added sugar; or they must be formulated to have specific health or wellness benefits; or they contain reduced calories or nutrients such as fat, sodium, or sugar. More than 100 PepsiCo products bear the Smart Spot logo of "Smart Choices Made Easy."

PepsiCo was committed to partnering Smart Spot with a nonprofit that focused on energy balance managed through healthy eating and physical activity. Serendipitously, during the spring of 2003, AOM

approached PepsiCo while it was searching for a partner. PepsiCo CEO
Steve Reineman, a fitness buff himself, had an early-adopter mentality
toward AOM's efforts. He liked the consumer focus on AOM's philos-
ophy, as well as helping people make small changes to improve their
lifestyles. He also had the right brands and the people to bring to the
table. Peters, Hill, and Reineman found that they were kindred spirits,
with visions that held a mutual attraction.

Clearly, sponsorship of AOM would positively affect the marketing
of the Smart Spot products, which had yet to launch. Conversely, with
the introduction of Smart Spot, PepsiCo could share in AOM's message
by giving people the tools they can use right now in the environment
we live in. "Anywhere in the United States, people have more healthy
options with Smart Spot products," noted AOM's Simonds, "allowing
them to make easier, healthier eating choices." Additionally, in partnering with PepsiCo, AOM hoped for a snowball effect, as once a big company is involved, others could follow.

PepsiCo agreed to join the effort as National Presenting Sponsor of
AOM. The partnership was formed over an eight-month process.
PepsiCo's Smart Spot line of products launched in February 2005.

Prior to the introduction of Smart Spot, in September 2004,
PepsiCo launched a new wellness benefit for employees and their
families. Called HealthRoads^{TM}, the program "partners with WebMD
and other selected companies and provides information, resources,
tools and incentives to encourage PepsiCo's employees and their families to live healthier lifestyles." The launch of PepsiCo's internal initiative gave further evidence of PepsiCo's commitment to health and
wellness, and met an important condition of its partnership with
AOM.

Ellen Taaffe, PepsiCo's Vice President of Marketing, Health, and
Wellness, led the development and launch of Smart Spot, in addition
to leading the PepsiCo sponsorship of AOM and the corporate kids
programming including Balance First^{TM}, elementary school and
middle school lesson plans teaching energy balance. In a presentation
at the "Environmental Solutions to Obesity in America's Youth"
conference in June 2005, she described Smart Spot as the "fastest
growing sector" and described her strategy as simple—to make a real
impact by offering consumers solutions that contribute to healthier

lifestyles (Environmental Health Perspectives, Volume 113, Number 8, August 2005).

Partnership Components

PepsiCo's contributions to AOM were much more than check-writing corporate philanthropy. As National Presenting Sponsor of AOM, PepsiCo provides funding in the form of unrestricted grants for grassroots efforts; expanded PepsiCo's Health and Wellness staff to do more under the Health and Wellness banner; created an educational program for elementary and middle-school children called Balance First, for which AOM is the program's key content provider; collaborates with its key media partner, the Discovery Channel, to create vignettes promoting AOM; facilitated AOM's partnerships with the National Urban League and the National Council of La Raza; and features AOM in Smart Spot messaging and promotion, including freestanding coupon inserts and pedometer giveaways for the launch of Smart Spot, as well as reciprocal links between the AOM and Smart Spot websites.

Perhaps the most ambitious element of the Smart Spot and AOM partnership was PepsiCo's sponsorship of AOM Day of Action, a national awareness event held on September 28, 2005, encouraging the American public to make AOM's two recommended small changes to their daily routine—2,000 more steps and 100 fewer calories—in order to prevent weight-related illnesses.

AOM and PepsiCo chose New York City as the venue for its flagship event. The plan: create a one-mile (approximately 2,000 steps) red-carpet path around a highly trafficked area in midtown Manhattan for the public and celebrities to walk in support of making small changes to create lasting wellness. To incentivize the public as well as the media, PepsiCo retained media personality Regis Philbin as the celebrity spokesperson to walk the red carpet, and secured the participation of Donald Trump (housed in nearby Trump Tower) for photo-ops.

AOM Day of Action participants received giveaways including a free AOM pedometer; Smart Spot products; a chance to win major league basketball tickets; and free blood-pressure screenings. Throughout the day, people also had the opportunity to "register" with AOM, which leveraged the event to launch its AOM Registry—the first

national database to track small lifestyle changes and how they contribute to better health.

Marketing support included AstraZeneca-funded television and
print advertisements with specific focus on the Latino market. Discovery ran vignettes with a PepsiCo/Smart Spot tie-in to drive AOM
Day of Action pledges. PepsiCo also funded a satellite media tour
featuring AOM's industry spokespersons.

Public relations support for AOM Day of Action included media
outreach efforts to garner advance and day-of print and electronic
coverage by national and local media. Additionally, PSAs were distributed to radio and television outlets nationwide for broadcast, and the
AOM Day of Action team provided appropriate training for AOM's
affiliates and partners—including the National Council of La Raza
and the National Urban League—to ensure maximum coverage of the
PSAs across the country and of AOM Day of Action.

Impact

Based on the increasing number of AOM users and recent public relations reporting, AOM's Simonds says she sees "a trend of increase in
awareness" toward AOM and its mission. She has observed that people
are coming to AOM via the Smart Spot website and product packaging, and states that several hundred thousand people had registered
with AOM prior to the Day of Action event. She also thinks that Smart
Spot's sponsorship of AOM, as "a private-public partnership that
works," has been educational for the media.

As a result of AOM day, the outcome in growth is impressive.
There were over 500,000 AOM participants, both online and offline.
There are more than 725 million media impressions to date, and
30,000 schools are reaching 123 million students while over 1,800
work sites are reaching 3.2 million employees. The age range by
decade is as follows: 4 percent fall under the age of 20; 14 percent fall
between the ages of 20 and 29; 23 percent fall between the ages of 30
and 39; 29 percent fall between the ages of 40 and 49; and 30 percent
are 50 years of age or older.

AOM's user success has reported that 71 percent of participants
maintained or lost weight, and 36 percent increased daily steps by 2,000
or even more.

Addressing Marketing Needs with an Array of Solutions

As you can see, by enhancing their reputation through CRM, PepsiCo's image issues were solved. Along with sponsoring AOM, PepsiCo began producing healthy food products, which led to a positive association. Because of its significant contributions to a healthful organization, PepsiCo is finally seen as a company that offers consumers nutritional options.

Through this CRM partnership, PepsiCo stands out from competitors, because unlike most of the latter, PepsiCo is now affiliated with health and nutrition.

Although the company may not have the problem of poor branding, its brand credibility is significantly enhanced because of its association with America on the Move, and its visibility all over the AOM website. This also relates to customer retention. When someone tracks their 2,000 steps, they see Smart Spot all over the AOM website. PepsiCo's visibility on all of the AOM materials both online and offline promotes the building of customer loyalty. As mentioned earlier, PepsiCo launched a new wellness benefit for employees and their families called HealthRoads. Through this program employee loyalty is met as well.

Through its myriad points-of-behavior reminders, AOM is looking toward future success by inspiring people to create lasting change—in the workplace, schools, and restaurants, from childhood on.

CHAPTER 7

BMW AND KOMEN FOUNDATION'S "ULTIMATE DRIVE" CASE STUDY

The Challenge

Breast cancer is the leading cancer site among American women and is second only to lung cancer in cancer deaths. At this time, there are slightly more than 2 million women living in the United States who have been diagnosed with and treated for breast cancer. It is the leading cause of cancer deaths among women ages 40–59. An estimated 211,240 new cases of invasive breast cancer were estimated among women in the U.S. during 2005. An estimated 40,870 women died from breast cancer in 2005. It is estimated that 1,690 men were diagnosed and 460 men died of breast cancer during 2005. Carcinoma in situ (CIS) will account for about 58,490 new cases this year (2005, American Cancer Society, Inc., Surveillance Research).

The Susan G. Komen Breast Cancer Foundation

The Susan G. Komen Breast Cancer Foundation was established in 1982 by Nancy Brinker to honor the memory of her sister, Susan G. Komen, who died from breast cancer at the age of 36. Considered the most progressive grassroots organization in breast cancer, the Komen Foundation is an international organization with a network of more than 75,000 active volunteers and 100 affiliates.

The Komen Foundation is the nation's largest private funder of breast cancer research and community outreach programs. Additionally, the foundation works to further its mission of eradicating breast cancer through research, education, screening, and treatment by providing local grants for such efforts for the medically underserved in communities across the U.S.

The Komen Foundation is also a leading nonprofit in the cause marketing arena: Its annual report indicates that the foundation raised $30 million in 2002 through CRM campaigns. The foundation counts among its largest corporate partners and programs Lee Jeans for Lee National Denim Day; Yoplait and the Save Lids to Save Lives program as well as the Komen "Race for the Cure" program; the Women's International Bowling Congress and the "Bowl for a Cure" program; and BMW North America and the "Ultimate Drive" promotion.

The Ultimate Drive

Charity Brands was approached by BMW and its marketing agency to identify and secure participation by an appropriate nonprofit in a fundraising promotion that could leverage grassroots support among volunteers.

The concept: a test drive with two caravans of 16 BMWs, one driving east and one driving west between participating BMW dealerships (a requirement of the partnership). For every mile driven, $1 is donated to a select NP.

Charity Brands first approached the American Heart Association, but the organization passed due to the active nature of the program (the necessity of driving from one location to the other in order to raise funds).

Charity Brands had a budding relationship with the Komen Foundation and approached it with the opportunity. The Komen Foundation expressed interest. (As it turned out, the Foundation had an existing relationship with BMW, but neither organization had the other on its radar.)

Due to the manpower needed to drive the cars, however, the program appeared cost-prohibitive. The solution: The Komen Foundation had a group of husbands of breast cancer survivors who were looking to donate their time and effort. Charity Brands proposed that these husbands drive the cars as their contribution.

We crafted the "Drive for the Cure" program plan that winter, and it was ratified by both parties in the spring. Upon approval, BMW implemented the program with its marketing agency.

The program surpassed all expectations, generating approximately $1.5 million for the Komen Foundation in the first year, and was renewed under the name "Ultimate Drive."

In the years since it was first designed, the "Ultimate Drive" promotion has grown to include more than 200 participating BMW centers nationwide and local events at each stop. Additionally, at each regional "Ultimate Drive" event a "Local Hero" (a community resident who has made an outstanding personal effort in the fight against breast cancer) is honored at an awards presentation. Each event kicks off with a survivor drive in which all vehicles parade through town driven by breast cancer survivors. For the 2005 campaign, BMW created specially designed merchandise for the Ultimate Drive to sell at each event.

All administrative costs of the "Ultimate Drive" program are underwritten by BMW separately and apart from the funds raised for this program.

Impact

To date, the "Ultimate Drive" has raised up to $1 million per year, and over $8 million for research in the past eight years. Additionally, the Komen Foundation's outreach efforts and early detection messages have touched the lives of hundreds of thousands of women and men.

In a conversation with the *Cause Marketing Forum*, Cindy Schneibel, VP of Cause Marketing for the Komen Foundation, commented that

> the dollars generated through Komen cause-related marketing programs increase our capacity to fund innovative breast cancer research and community outreach programs. In addition to raising funds, these programs increase awareness about breast health and breast cancer, educate consumers about a variety of breast cancer issues, encourage consumer activism and bring in more volunteers. As a volunteer-driven organization, this is a tremendous asset to an organization like Komen. (http://www.komen.org)

Addressing Marketing Needs with an Array of Solutions

In the case of BMW's association with the Komen Foundation, hyper competition and efficient access to market interweave. BMW was clever enough to realize that women make up about 50 percent of the buying decisions when it comes to purchasing a new vehicle. BMW's involvement with the Komen Foundation directly targeted these women consumers. By holding this annual event, BMW solidified its customer retention rate. The public events held at various dealerships helped develop customer loyalty to the brand, as well as associating BMW employees as good corporate citizens within these communities.

CHAPTER 8

THE FIGHT AGAINST CARDIOVASCULAR DISEASE CASE STUDY

The Challenge

For decades, cardiovascular disease (CVD) was the number-one cause of death in the United States, surpassing mortality rates from cancer, accidents, and HIV (AIDS) combined. (Cancer was recently identified as the new number-one killer in the U.S. by a slight margin.) The American Heart Association estimates that CVD claimed nearly 927,450 lives in 2002—38 percent of all deaths or 1 of every 2.6 deaths. Approximately 70.1 million Americans were faced with one or more forms of CVD in 2002, including high blood pressure (65 million); coronary heart disease (such as acute heart attacks and angina pectoris) (13 million); and strokes (6.4 million). And although death rates from CVD declined 18 percent from 1992 to 2002, in the same ten-year period the actual number of deaths increased 0.8 percent. However, along with organizations like the AHA and programs such as heart-check, the Pharmaceutical Roundtable, Heart Walk, the Daily Health Tips in *The Wall St. Journal*, and Jump Rope for Heart—heart-related organizations are continually raising money for research, as well as building awareness.

The American Heart Association

The AHA is the nation's largest and most strongly supported voluntary health organization. The AHA's mission is to reduce death and disability from cardiovascular diseases and stroke. The organization, founded by cardiologists in 1924, aims to discover new knowledge through research and provide information to consumers about effective ways to prevent and treat CVD.

Heart-Check

Backed by decades of research proving that healthy food habits can help reduce high blood cholesterol, high blood pressure, excessive body weight, and the risk of stroke, in 1995 the AHA created a new strategy to help Americans combat CVD with the heart-check certification program, developed in conjunction with the Food and Drug Administration (FDA) to help consumers identify and select heart-healthy, nutritious foods while grocery shopping.

Products eligible for heart-check certification must first meet nutritional guidelines established by the FDA. These guidelines dictate that heart-check-eligible foods must be low in fat, saturated fat, and cholesterol. Specifically, the AHA notes that

> . . . the reference amount (i.e., standard serving size established by the U.S. government) may include up to 3 grams or less of total fat, 1 gram or less of saturated fat and 20 milligrams or less of cholesterol. The product must not exceed a sodium disqualifying level and must include at least 10 percent of the Daily Value per Reference Amount of at least one of six nutrients: protein, dietary fiber, vitamin A, vitamin C, calcium or iron.
>
> The nutritional guidelines for seafood, game meats (both governed by the FDA), and meat and poultry products (governed by the USDA) require that a product be "extra lean." That means it must contain less than 5 grams of total fat, less than 2 grams of saturated fat and less than 95 milligrams of cholesterol per reference amount and per 100 grams. The product must not exceed a sodium disqualifying level. (http://www.americanheart.org)

The AHA established several additional rules beyond the FDA's framework. First, the organization applied the "Jellybean Rule" to products—that is products must have some nutritional value to receive certification. Medical foods, dietary supplements, or alcoholic beverages do not qualify for certification. Second, the AHA would not work with companies that are owned by or own 5 percent or more of a tobacco company. Therefore, companies like Kraft (owned by Phillip Morris, now called Altria Group) are immediately disqualified from being able to use the heart-check symbol on their products.

Additionally, heart-check certification is restricted to food products that are distributed solely within the United States and its territories and possessions. The certification program also excludes restaurants, and the heart-check symbol may not be used in connection with recipes, sweepstakes, or any certification program fundraising promotions.

The Certification Process

To receive the heart-check certification, food manufacturers must submit the products, their nutritional information, written assurances of eligibility, and a contractual agreement to the AHA for review.

Additionally, the AHA's fee for heart-check certification is $7,500 per product (with $4,500 per product for annual renewals and volume discounts). The AHA notes that the fee "covers the administration of the program; nutritional packaging, promotional, science and legal reviews; and other activities that maintain the program integrity." The AHA gains no profit from the manufacturer fees.

The AHA hired the author's company, Charity Brands, to develop the partnership component of the certification program. The Charity Brands team orchestrated a plan that made heart-check certification both a promotional opportunity and an obligation for participants. Should a food manufacturer receive heart-check certification for any of its products, it was required to include the heart-check logo in all marketing and promotional programs and materials, according to specific AHA guidelines. This created a winning benefit for both partners: food manufacturers received credibility and customer loyalty through AHA/heart-check signage, promotions, and community outreach programs, and the AHA gained greater reach in its campaign to educate consumers and encourage them to make better dietary choices.

Building Relationships

General Mills was one of the first companies to feature the heart-check in an advertising campaign, for Cheerios. The campaign was a huge success, as General Mills attributed the product's 4 percent growth (in a flat cereal market) to the heart-check symbol and messaging on-pack and in its advertising. Based on this success, I knew we had a strong program with which to build significant reach for AHA and healthy eating messaging.

I then took an "outside of the box" view of the heart-check program and worked with the AHA to make two major domestic commodities eligible for heart-check certification: milk and citrus fruit.

I approached the International Dairy Foods Association (IDFA) the governing body of 2,500 member dairies in the United States alone, with a plan to certify certain milk products. The IDFA appeared to be open to ideas, though somewhat resistant. I proposed using three dairies in a pilot program for 1/2 percent or skim milk products. The IDFA agreed, and the pilot program was implemented. The program was a resounding success, creating a snowball effect among the other member dairies that then wanted to be a part of the heart-check certification program. The pilot program resulted in the AHA signing a ten-year contract with the IDFA, representing all of their member dairies.

As a result, the relationship between AHA-IDFA and Charity Brands harvested the famous milk mustache ads that were created for skim milk and 1/2 percent milk with the heart-check symbol featured in each advertisement. The first ad featured singer Tony Bennett. Since then, many famous personalities—from Ron Howard, Martha Stewart, Naomi Campbell, Conan O'Brian, and Whoopi Goldberg to Serena Williams, Joss Stone, Stockard Channing, and Kelly Clarkson—have supported the initiative by appearing in these advertisements.

In approaching the citrus fruit industry, I was faced with the challenge of navigating through the complex waters of such organizations as the Florida Department of Citrus (FDOC). I collaborated with Edelman Fleischman and Hilliard (FDOC's public relations team) and presented a heart-check certification proposal for fresh-squeezed Florida grapefruit juice, which was approved.

Once certification was granted, I engineered the plan to get AHA approval for heart-check signage on bins and in promotional materials (in addition to having the symbol on product packaging). With approval for heart-check signage on bins granted, citrus fruit growers could use the heart-check symbol and sell that leverage to Tropicana.

After making these gains, I approached Tropicana with a program that gave the company products the heart-check symbol and included a travel promotion component that would benefit the AHA. An on-pack offer to receive up to $5,000 in savings on a wide range of travel programs such as cruises, flights, hotel accommodations, etc. was included along with discounts at attractions all over the country. Because of this offer, AHA garnered millions of additional impressions.

Today, products with the heart-check symbol enjoy a very strong presence in the marketplace. The heart-check symbol is seen on hundreds of leading food products including beverages; breakfast foods and cereals; dairy products; frozen foods; fruits and vegetables; general groceries; meat and poultry (canned, fresh, frozen, deli-style); meat substitutes; pasta and pasta sauces; and seafood.

As of this printing, the following food manufacturers are participants in the AHA's heart-check certification program:

Heart-Check Food Manufacturers

- Adler Seeds
- Allen Canning Company
- Archer Daniels Midland Company
- Atlanta Corporation; Beef Packers Inc.
- Beefmaster Cattlemen, L.P.
- Bimbo Bakeries USA
- Boar's Head Provision Company, Inc.
- Bruce Foods Corporation
- Bryan Foods, Inc.
- Cacique, Inc.
- Campbell Soup Company
- Campbell Soup Company–Pepperidge Farm, Inc.
- Chiquita Brands Company
- Clearwater Fine Foods Inc.
- Clougherty Packing Company
- ConAgra Dairy Foods
- ConAgra Food Service
- ConAgra Frozen Foods
- ConAgra Grocery Foods
- ConAgra Refrigerated Foods
- ConAgra Retail Foods
- Conopco, Inc.
- Crider, Inc.
- Cutler at Abbeville, LLC
- Deni's Sauce Company, LLC
- El Aguila Food Products, Inc.
- Empire Kosher Poultry, Inc.
- Excel Corporation
- Excel Corporation–Taylor Packing Co., Inc.
- Fairbank Farms
- Farmland Industries, Inc.–Farmland Foods
- Fieldale Farms Corporation
- Florida's Natural Growers

(continued)

Heart-Check Food Manufacturers (*Continued*)

- Foster Poultry Farm; Frito-Lay, Inc.
- Fruiticana
- General Mills, Inc.
- General Mills, Inc.–8th Continent, LLC
- GFA Brands, Inc.
- Glenn Foods, Inc.
- Gold Kist, Inc.
- Hodgson Mill, Inc.
- Hormel Foods Corporation
- Indiana Packers Corp.
- Integrated Bakery Resources, Inc.
- International Dairy Foods Association
- Interstate Brands Corporation
- John Hofmeister & Son, Inc.
- John Morrell & Co.
- Kansas City Steak Company
- Kashi Company
- Kellogg USA, Inc.
- KFP International, Ltd.
- Laguna Tuna, LLC
- Laura's Lean Beef Company
- LiDestri Foods, Inc.
- Lido Veal & Lamb, Inc.
- LifeForce-Labs, Inc.
- M & I Seafood Manufacturing Inc.
- Malt-O-Meal Company
- Maple Leaf Consumer Foods
- Marcho Farms, Inc.
- Maverick Ranch Association
- Meijer, Inc.
- Milton's Baking Company
- Morningstar Foods Inc.
- Murray's Free Roaming Chicken, Inc.
- MW Polar Foods
- National Watermelon Promotion Board
- Naturade, Inc.
- Nature's Path Foods USA, Inc.
- New World Pasta Company
- Nonna's Kitchen
- North American Beverage Company
- Nulaid Foods Inc.
- Old Orchard Brands LLC
- Packerland Processing Co., Inc.
- Papetti's Hygrade Egg Products, Inc.
- Pilgrim's Pride Corporation
- Pink Lady USA, LLC
- Pinnacle Foods Corporation
- POM Wonderful, LLC
- Rader Farms, Inc.
- Ralcorp Holdings, Inc. (Ralston Foods Division)
- Seaboard Farms, Inc.
- Sealord North America, Inc.
- Setton International Foods, Inc.
- Shapiro Packing Company
- Smithfield Packing Company
- Springerhill Ranch Meat Products
- Starkist Seafood Company
- Stockmasters, Inc.
- Stone Meats, Inc.
- Swift Foods dba Swift & Company
- The B. Manischewitz Company, LLC
- The Baker
- The Coca-Cola Company

(continued)

Heart-Check Food Manufacturers (*Continued*)

- The Coca-Cola Company–Brain Twist
- The Dannon Company
- The Hain Celestial Group, Inc.
- The Kroger Company
- The Kroger Company–King Sooperes
- The Quaker Oats Company
- The Quaker Oats Company–Frito Lay Quaker Puerto Rico
- Tony Downs Foods Company
- Tree Top, Inc.
- Tropicana Products, Inc.
- Tumaro's Inc.
- Turkey Hill Dairy
- Tyson Foods, Inc.
- Tyson Fresh Meats
- Ungar's Food Products, Inc.
- United Food Group, LLC
- Vermont Bread Company
- Welch Foods, Inc.
- Yoo-Hoo Chocolate Beverage Corporation

Pharmaceutical Roundtable

In 1997, Charity Brands helped revamp a program for the American Heart Association called the Pharmaceutical Roundtable (PRT). The PRT is a strategic coalition of eight leading pharmaceutical companies and association volunteers. It was formed in 1988 through a partnership with eight original founding members that each committed to a five-year membership term and contributed money annually to support AHA research and educational programs. The eight founding members were

- Bristol–Myers Company
- CIBA–GEIGY Corporation
- Genentech, Inc.
- Sandoz Pharmaceuticals Corporation
- Sanofi Winthrop Pharmaceuticals
- Squibb Corporation
- Wyeth–Ayerst Laboratories
- Boehringer Ingelheim Pharmaceuticals, Inc.

These visionary companies made a commitment to a truly novel concept at the time—the AHA's PRT was the first roundtable in the pharmaceutical industry.

In 1997, the AHA asked Charity Brands to examine how to further its mission and better serve the needs of the healthcare system through the PRT. While PRT member contributions helped narrow the research gap, more funds were needed to ensure that meritorious projects received the support they deserved. In response to this need, Charity Brands redesigned the PRT to generate additional research dollars and provide members with benefits that would enable them to better educate consumers and professionals on cardiovascular health issues.

The concept was to create a world-class pharmaceutical roundtable with programs and benefits to command multiple-year commitments and significant revenue. The difficulty lay in the ten-year history of annual low-fee commitments, few benefits, and an overall unhappy membership. However, recreating the PRT with a three-pronged approach—an elevated research commitment, a consumer compliance initiative, and "best available" marketing benefits for reaching healthcare professionals and consumers—made it a more viable and substantial forum, and a more profitable one.

Through Charity Brands, PRT received instant gratification. By co-branding promotional opportunities, garnering larger funds for research, allowing members Scientific Sessions Conference privileges, creating collaborative marketing and professional educational programs, and giving priority consideration for program sponsorship, the PRT became an overall bigger and better initiative. Without these funds, potentially lifesaving breakthroughs in research would go unsupported.

With Charity Brands's help, the PRT successfully became a unique forum that allows members of the pharmaceutical industry to band together and pursue common goals. Its most important objective is to improve the overall cardiovascular health of the United States. By raising money for research, patient education, and public and professional informational sessions, the PRT is able to reach millions of individuals suffering from heart-related diseases, as well as anyone generally concerned about their heart health.

American Heart Walk

Charity Brands's relationship with the AHA yielded numerous successes for not only the heart-check certification program and the Pharmaceutical Roundtable, but also AHA's American Heart Walk, the organization's annual walking event held regionally across the

United States. Heart Walk encourages individuals and their families to live a healthy lifestyle and engage in physical activity. In 2005, over 1 million walkers participated in more than 600 events across the country, raising funds to save lives from heart-related diseases.

In the late '90s, ConAgra (the manufacturer of Healthy Choice products) was the national sponsor of the American Health Walk. ConAgra wanted to rescind its sponsorship due to strategic changes within the company. AHA was initially inclined to allow the company to cancel the contract; however, I felt there was a way to satisfy ConAgra's change in direction and keep them as a national sponsor of AHA, but more about that later.

We spent several weeks developing a new sponsorship package and new sponsorship benefits for Heart Walk, and then took it on the road. One of my first contacts with the new sponsorship opportunity was the president of Archer Daniels Midland. Together we crafted a three-year deal making the company a national sponsor of AHA's Heart Walk. The deal was finalized and approved very quickly after AHA was satisfied that ADM's past management challenges were behind it. The AHA received $1.5 million in cash each year for three years, plus $10–20 million in advertisements. This was the first national sponsorship that Charity Brands Marketing secured.

After ADM served for six years as the national sponsor for the Heart Walk, SUBWAY took an interest and came on board as the second national sponsor. SUBWAY then subsequently took on national sponsorship of "Jump Rope for Heart"—AHA's elementary school fundraising event.

The Wall Street Journal Daily Health Tips

So what happened to ConAgra? The company wanted to withdraw its sponsorship of the Heart Walk because it wanted more visibility for the company and its Healthy Choice brand among the investment community. As a result, my team and I proposed a "Health Tip of the Day" consumer education program, with placement on page A-4 of *The Wall Street Journal* (a coveted piece of real estate and an ambitious plan that was unheard of at the time). The proposal was a success: With Charity Brands's reconfigured sponsorship appealing to ConAgra, the AHA kept ConAgra on as national program sponsor and actually increased both its revenue and reach due to the nature of the health tips program.

As you might have guessed, the idea was extremely successful. *The Wall Street Journal* worked perfectly in conjunction with the AHA and its message of heart health because of its at-risk readers. The newspaper targets male readers over the age of 35, which is the foremost group at risk of heart attack or other cardiovascular complications.

The Wall Street Journal Daily Health and Nutrition Tips generated over 59.5 million estimated impressions for 1997–1998. This program constantly showcased ConAgra's relationship with the AHA to millions of health-conscious decision makers every day. The current *Wall Street Journal* readership is estimated at over 5 million individuals, with the number increasing daily. The health and nutrition tips provided multimedia global reach for AHA nutritional messages and ConAgra products. ConAgra further distinguished itself and the AHA with the overwhelming success of health segments on *CBS This Morning.* This strategic media partnership provided millions of consumers with key health messages and practical tools needed to improve their health by offering important, timely information concerning nutrition, total health, wellness, and other related subjects.

As a result of ConAgra's success, AstraZeneca teamed up with AHA to do the same type of media campaign—this time focusing on blood pressure. AstraZeneca was trying to promote its drug for hypertension at the time, and this was a perfect launching ground for the campaign. Daily health tips were called "Pressure Points" and offered Americans practical advice on how to take care of their blood pressure. The daily "Pressure Point" tips were also featured on the AztraZeneca website.

Addressing Marketing Needs with an Array of Solutions

As you can see, we helped the American Heart Association develop or adapt its sponsorship programs to meet many of the needs and solutions referred to in Chapter 2. Through the many programs, the AHA has provided a manifold of solutions to marketers' needs.

Sponsors' image and credibility issues are addressed through alignment with AHA as a recognized and respected voluntary health organization. The heart-check program offers product differentiation and gives efficient access to the growing number of health-conscious consumers by introducing people to a simple way to make healthier food selections. The PRT enables drug manufacturers to effectively and efficiently communicate with the health-care system through an additional channel, and Heart Walk provides sponsors with visibility among family gatekeepers (moms) at both the national and grassroots levels. Finally, *The Wall Street Journal* programs allowed companies to communicate directly with a highly targeted audience segment that is interested in health for themselves and for investment purposes.

Over the course of a ten-year relationship, Charity Brands Charity Brands Marketing helped the AHA establish a portfolio of programs that has garnered millions of dollars for research, and has also significantly helped Americans understand much more about heart disease.

CHAPTER 9

THE EVOLUTION OF SMOKING CASE STUDY

According to the Centers for Disease Control and Prevention, cigarette smoking is the leading cause of preventable death in the United States, claiming the lives of approximately 440,000 people each year. The Centers estimate that 22.5 percent (46 million) of adults smoke cigarettes, with 28.5 percent of these smokers between 18 and 24 years old; 25.7 percent between 25 and 44 years old; 22.7 percent between 45 and 64 years old; and 9.3 percent age 65 or older.

The tobacco industry has undergone many significant changes over the past 40 years. However slow, the anti-smoking movement has gained significant ground without much corporate support beyond that of pharmaceutical companies. Although arguably in the best interest of the public, very few corporations have been willing to support the act of quitting. However, even without their support, individuals all over the world have banded together to create campaigns and messages of nonsmoking. These groups, along with the media, have been powerful advocates of tobacco control. Because of these influences, even without the support of the corporate world, we can see a significant social change within our culture.

The Great American Smokeout

The American Cancer Society pioneered national anti-smoking campaigns with the Great American Smokeout. The event, which encourages people to stop smoking for one day, grew out of a 1971 event in Randolph, Massachusetts, in which former high school guidance counselor Arthur P. Mullaney asked people to give up cigarettes for one day and donate the money they would have spent on cigarettes to a scholarship fund. Then, in 1974, former *Monticello Times* editor Lynn R. Smith spearheaded Minnesota's first "D-Day," or "Don't Smoke Day." As the effort was building momentum, the California Division of the American Cancer Society (ACS) adopted the idea. In November 1976, the organization succeeded in getting almost 1 million smokers to quit for the day. The ACS then expanded the campaign, and the first national Great American Smokeout was held in 1977. According to www.quitsmoking.com, as many as one-third of the nation's 46 million smokers stop smoking during the Great American Smokeout traditionally held each November.

Each year during the Great American Smokeout, the ACS sponsors local and nationwide activities and special events to promote the benefits of non-smoking. The countless festivities are supported by thousands of ACS volunteers who help publicize the events and distribute information about quitting smoking to schools, malls, and workplaces nationwide. The Great American Smokeout is also promoted by a sophisticated national marketing plan of print and television advertisements, as well as media outreach and editorial coverage.

The Centers for Disease Control notes in a 1997 report on the impact of the 1996 Great American Smokeout

- "The 1996 Great American Smokeout paid advertisements reached an estimated 122 million adults, including 30 million smokers—nearly two of every three smokers in the United States."
- "The percentage of smokers who reported either quitting or reducing smoking for one day increased from 18% in 1995 to 26% in 1996, possibly the direct result of the national Great American Smokeout promotion."
- "On the day of the 1996 Great American Smokeout, 26% of smokers (an increase from 18% in 1995) either quit or reduced their smoking for the day,"
- "In 1996, sales of nicotine medications increased by 11% over average sales during the four-week national Great American Smokeout promotion; sales during the specific week of Great American Smokeout increased 30%" (http://www.cdc.gov/ tobacco/research_data/advcoadv/mmwr4637.htm).

In addition to creating awareness of the dangers of tobacco use and galvanizing the American public to make efforts to quit or reduce smoking, the Great American Smokeout has played a critical role in influencing anti-smoking research and landmark policies.

Prior to the Great American Smokeout, the ACS sparked a snowball effect of anti-smoking efforts and policies with its 1954 Hammond-Horn study, which demonstrated the correlation between cigarette smoking and mortality rates. The study was followed by a 1964 report by the Surgeon General, which led to Congress passing the Federal Cigarette Labeling and Advertising Act, requiring health warnings on all cigarette packages. In 1970, tobacco advertisements were banned from television and radio.

Masters Settlement Agreement

The tobacco industry suffered its most crushing blow on November 23, 1998, when the Masters Settlement Agreement (MSA)—a landmark agreement between 11 tobacco companies and 46 states, five territories, and the District of Columbia—was reached. The largest settlement in history, the MSA determined that the tobacco industry should pay $264 billion over a period of 25 years to the U.S. states and territories to compensate for tobacco-related healthcare costs.

The tobacco companies were also subject to sweeping marketing and advertising restrictions; youth access restrictions; smoking cessation and prevention measures; lobbying and civil liability restrictions; and pubic disclosure regarding tobacco products. The agreement does not outline rules for the Internet, and does not ban print advertisements.

The *Chronicle of Higher Education* noted in its March 18, 2005 issue (Section: Students, Volume 51, Issue 28, Page A34) that "the industry responded to the new rules by spending more on marketing to 'entry level' smokers—those ages 18 to 24. In 2002 alone, the marketing budgets of the 11 companies exceeded $12.5 billion, an 81% increase from the $6.9 billion they spent in the year before the settlement, according to the Federal Trade Commission."

American Legacy Foundation

The American Legacy Foundation (ALF) is a 501(c)(3) organization that was founded in March 1999 as a result of the MSA, and is funded primarily by payments designated by the settlement. With the mission "to build a world where young people reject tobacco and anyone can quit," the independent public health foundation "develops national programs that address the health effects of tobacco use through grants, technical training and assistance, youth activism, strategic partnerships, counter-marketing and grass roots marketing campaigns, public relations, research and community outreach to populations disproportionately affected by the toll of tobacco" (http://www.americanlegacy.org). Citing that approximately 80 percent of smokers begin using tobacco before age 18, the AHL placed primary focus on this segment of society to reduce smoking rates. ALF's two-pronged goal is to outfit American youth with the tools to reject tobacco, and to "eliminate disparities in access to tobacco prevention and cessation services."

The ALF has experienced enormous success with its teen-oriented truth® campaign—an advertising, grassroots, and online initiative to prevent youth smoking. Since its inception in February 2000, this campaign has become the largest youth smoking prevention campaign in the country and has helped reduce youth smoking rates. According to the ALF, the "Monitoring the Future" survey, sponsored by the National Institute on Drug Abuse and conducted by the University of Michigan, "reported dramatic declines in smoking rates among 8th, 10th and 12th graders, citing truth® as a factor in this public health success story." The ALF also cites research published in the March issue of the *American Journal of Public Health* that in 2002 there were 300,000 fewer youth smokers because of this campaign.

The truth® advertising campaign targets print, radio, the Internet, and television, especially youth-oriented outlets such as MTV, the WB, and UPN. Its grassroots initiative sees teens spreading the word about the dangers of tobacco use in peer-to-peer settings. The ALF notes that the truth® summer grassroots initiative has reached thousands of youths across the United States since its inception in 2000, and its truth® website receives thousands of hits each day.

The ALF also targets youth culture via its Youth Advisory Panel (providing insight and perspective); Speakers Bureau (offering presentations to schools, conferences, and organizations around the country); and Project 2030 Internship Program (giving youth the opportunity to work with professionals in the tobacco control and prevention movement).

Women and Smoking

Marketing via the media has not always encouraged quitting tobacco. Our youth have been a target of tobacco companies in the past, especially females. Teenage girls often begin to smoke to avoid gaining weight and to identify themselves as independent and glamorous. Social images and advertisements can convince teens that being slightly overweight is worse than smoking.

According to the Center for Disease Control and Prevention, over the years women have been a primary target in the marketing of tobacco products. Many tobacco companies have aimed their advertising toward women, as well as producing brands specifically to appeal to the female population. Lucky Strike, Virginia Slims, and Capri's are just a few of the brands designed to stimulate a woman's interest in smoking.

In 1920, an advertisement ran for the Spud brand of cigarettes with the slogan, "To read the advertisements these days, a fellow'd think the pretty girls do all the smoking." Unfortunately, this was not the only product that chose to objectify women in their advertising. Lucky Strike spawned the message, "Reach for a Lucky instead of a sweet!," blatantly implying a connection between smoking and weight control. However, because of this strategy, Lucky Strike brand increased its sales 300 percent in the first year of its campaign.

In the 1990s, Philip Morris marketed Virginia Slims cigarettes to women by utilizing the rising women's movements. With slogans like "You've come a long way baby" and "It's a woman thing," it was difficult not to make the connection between smoking and women's empowerment. Not only are the advertisements themselves marketed for women, so is the appearance of the actual cigarette. According to Wikipedia, Virginia Slims are narrower, 21 mm in circumference, than ordinary cigarettes, which measure 25 mm. Capri Slims are even "slimmer" at 17 mm in circumference. Both of these brands are longer than the average cigarette in order to impart a more graceful appearance and to presumably decrease the amount of smoke they produce. In the past, Philip Morris has also offered discounts on food, milk, soft drinks, and laundry detergent with the purchase of its tobacco products.

Cigarette smoking has proven to have many harmful effects on women's health. An estimated 17.3 percent of pregnant women aged

15–44 years smoke cigarettes, compared with 31.1 percent of nonpregnant women of the same age. According to the CDC, smoking can increase the risk of infertility, preterm delivery, stillbirth, low birth weight, and sudden infant death syndrome. Not only does smoking cigarettes risk defects in the unborn, women who smoke are more susceptible to diseases such as cancer of the lung, oral cavity, pharynx, larynx, esophagus, pancreas, kidney, bladder, and uterus. Women who smoke are also at increased risk of heart disease and chronic lung disease. An estimated 178,000 women die annually because of smoking.

Effects on Minority Groups

Not only are women at an increased risk for tobacco-related disease, but certain minority groups are at a higher risk as well. The threat of lung cancer, tuberculosis, premature childbirth, and asthma are higher for these groups. Rates of cancers related to cigarette smoking vary widely among members of ethnic groups, but are generally highest in African American men. For instance, according to the American Lung Association, African Americans suffer from many chronic and preventable diseases associated with smoking. Compared to Caucasian Americans, African Americans are at increased risk for many lung conditions primarily caused or worsened by tobacco smoking.

Like women, minority groups are specifically targeted through advertising. For instance, research suggests that three popular African American magazines, *Ebony, Jet,* and *Essence,* receive significantly higher profits than most mainstream publications due to the frequency of their tobacco-related advertisements. Currently, the Brown and Williamson Tobacco Corporation is aiming its Kool cigarette campaign at African American youths by including hip-hop characters in their advertisements. Furthermore, certain tobacco products are marketed toward Hispanics and Native Americans by promoting brands of cigarettes with names such as Rio, Dorado, and American Spirit. The tobacco industry has also sponsored festivals geared toward Asian American Heritage Month.

According to the 2003 National Health Interview Survey, 22.8 percent of the general adult population smokes (25.2 percent of men and 20.7 percent of women). Among white adults, 24 percent total smoke

(25.4 percent of men and 22.8 percent of women). A total of 22.3 percent of black adults smoke (27.7 percent of men and 17.9 percent of women).

Perhaps the lack of education is a factor in the lives of individuals who smoke. Among African Americans, as with other U.S. populations, the prevalence of smoking declines as education level increases. In 2002, smoking rates were over three times higher among African American males who had less than a high school education (37.9 percent) compared to those with a college education (11.3 percent). Smoking rates are also higher in African American females who have less than a high school education (26.3 percent) compared to those with a college education (11.6 percent).

Among Hispanics, a total of 16.7 percent smoke (21.6 percent of men, and 11.9 percent of women). While the figures for Hispanics are lower than the national average, this is due mainly to the extraordinarily small proportion of Hispanic women who report current smoking. Among Native Americans and Alaskan natives, 32.7 percent total smoke (33.5 percent of men and 31.7 percent of women).

According to the ALA, the overall number of Caucasians who smoke has been on a decline, increasing the number of tobacco advertisements geared toward minorities. Advertisements include magazines, strategically located billboards, and tobacco company sponsorship of entertainment and athletic events.

It is vital that we target minorities in our attempt to reduce tobacco smoking, as well as our youth. Certain organizations like the American Legacy Foundation have begun to target minority groups or "priority populations," which are considered "under-served communities that have disproportionate health burdens from tobacco use and often have less access to smoking cessation and prevention services (http://www.nwlc.org/pdf/LegacyFactSheet.pdf). The Priority Populations Initiative has funneled $21 million in grants over three years to organizations that work to reduce the overall cost of tobacco use on populations including African American, Asian American/Pacific Islander, gay/lesbian/bisexual/transgender, Hispanic/Latino, low socioeconomic, Native American/Alaska Native, and mental health/substance abuse.

World Conference on Tobacco Health

In 2000, Charity Brands was hired by the 11th World Conference on Tobacco Health to manage sponsorship sales for the conference, which was held August 6–10 in Chicago—the first time in 25 years that the conference was held in the U.S. The conference allowed organizations and individuals to band together to increase international leadership in the fight against tobacco. The goal of the conference was to turn the pressure of smoking into the prevention of smoking—for youth, women, minorities, and all of the individuals affected.

The conference was officially hosted by the American Cancer Society, along with the American Medical Association and the Robert Wood Johnson Foundation. Co-sponsoring nonprofits also included the Centers for Disease Control and Prevention, the American Heart Association, the American Lung Association, and the National Cancer Institute. The World Health Organization (WHO) and a number of other international and national health groups also served as conference partners.

Charity Brands exceeded sponsorship sales goals by 25 percent, achieving nearly $3 million in sales. Approximately 3,500 health leaders and professionals attended the conference. Charity Brands was subsequently hired to sell sponsorships for the national conference.

Additionally, Charity Brands played an instrumental role in building the relationship between the ALF, its truth® campaign, and the American Cancer Association, which resulted in the "Kids Track" program spearheaded by the ALF.

Philip Morris/Altria Group

Altria Group is the parent company of Kraft Foods, Philip Morris International, Philip Morris USA, and Philip Morris Capital Corporation. Altria Group is also the largest shareholder in the world's second-largest brewer, SABMiller, with a 33.9 percent economic interest.

Each of the Altria Group subsidiaries executes cause-related initiatives, from nutrition, health, and wellness and sustainable coffee/cocoa activities (Kraft) to "responsible marketing initiatives" and support for MSA-mandated tobacco regulation.

After the MSA was made, Philip Morris went on the offense to protect its image and profits—an exorbitantly expensive effort that backfired, as the 2000 *Cone/Roper Executive Study* explains:

> *Consumers want to know which companies are doing what, but if a company is perceived as exaggerating or hiding something, they can be punished. A case in point is Philip Morris. After the tobacco lawsuits, Philip Morris launched an aggressive public relations campaign that included TV spots about the company's charitable work. Word quickly spread that the advertising campaign was rumored to be more expensive than the money being spent on charity. A subsequent Harris poll found that 16 percent of respondents were still boycotting Philip Morris despite the $100 million plus campaign. (http://www.coneinc.com)*

Since then, Philip Morris has sought to bury its past and craft an image as a good corporate citizen. The December 19, 2004 article by Myron Levin in the *Los Angeles Times* article states:

> *. . . the company and its parent, Altria Group Inc., have moved aggressively to separate themselves from the rest of the tobacco industry. Philip Morris has spent $500 million over the last five years on programs to fight underage smoking, such as paying incentives to retailers to keep cigarettes behind the counter. The company's TV commercials state flatly that smoking is dangerous and addictive. Altria is the only major tobacco company to voluntarily stop advertising its brands in magazines. And it has broken ranks with its competitors by joining top health and anti-smoking groups in seeking authority for the Food and Drug Administration to regulate tobacco products. Long known for charitable giving, Altria has donated about $60 million this year to 1,200 nonprofit groups involved in its pet causes: the arts, hunger relief and curbing domestic violence.*

The article goes on to note, however:

> *. . . many aren't buying Altria's new look. Tobacco foes—and some neutral observers—say there's a disconnect between the image it presents and the way Altria makes its living as the world's largest and most successful marketer of a deadly product. They contend that the company still promotes its brands in foreign markets by methods long banished here. And they say that in the U.S., the company continues to resist measures that would cut the death toll from smoking.*

What the States Are Doing About the MSA

Since the 1998 state tobacco settlement, the Campaign for Tobacco-Free Kids has issued regular reports assessing whether the states are keeping their promise to use their settlement funds—expected to total $246 billion over 25 years—to attack the enormous public health problem posed by tobacco use. The organization's 2005 report that was conducted in association with the American Heart Association, American Cancer Society, and American Lung Association, found that "most states are failing to keep this promise even as they collect record amounts of revenue from the tobacco settlement and tobacco taxes and even as the tobacco companies spend record amounts to market their deadly and addictive products."

Among the findings detailed in the report:

- "Only three states—Maine, Delaware and Mississippi— currently fund tobacco prevention programs at minimum levels recommended by the U.S. Centers for Disease Control and Prevention (CDC). Thirty-seven states and the District of Columbia fund such programs at less than half the CDC minimum or provide no state funding at all."
- "The states have cut funding for tobacco prevention programs by 28% over the last three years and collectively have budgeted $538 million for tobacco prevention this year, which is only a third of what the CDC recommends."
- "In contrast, tobacco companies have increased their annual marketing expenditures to a record $12.7 billion a year, according to the Federal Trade Commission. This means the tobacco companies spend more than $23 to market cigarettes and other tobacco products in the U.S. for every dollar the states spend on programs to protect kids from tobacco."
- "The tobacco companies spend more on marketing in a single day—at least $34 million—than 46 states and the District of Columbia spend in an entire year on tobacco prevention. Tobacco companies spend more in a single hour—$1.4 million—than nine states and DC spend on tobacco prevention annually.

- "States have cut funding for tobacco prevention despite collecting a record $20 billion this year in tobacco-generated revenue from the tobacco settlement and tobacco taxes. State tobacco revenues have skyrocketed because 38 states and DC have increased tobacco taxes in the past three years, some more than once. It would take just eight percent of the states' total tobacco revenue to fund tobacco prevention programs in every state at CDC-recommended levels."

(*A Broken Promise to Our Children, the 1998 State Tobacco Settlement Seven Years Later.* November 30, 2005)

A Look into Our Future

According to the CDC in the four decades following the release of that first Surgeon General's Report on smoking and health in 1950, we have seen dramatic progress in reducing tobacco use in this country. It is likely that the media will continue to encourage the act of quitting, and tobacco companies will become less and less powerful. As we can see now, even Philip Morris boasts of its "responsible marketing" on its website. If tobacco companies are selling and producing products that they discourage forthrightly, perhaps smoking will gradually become less of an issue. Not only is the message of nonsmoking more and more prevalent in the media, we can also see the effort of individuals who have changed laws surrounding the smoking issue from states like New York and California banning smoking in all public places. In 2003, the UK banned the advertising and promotion of tobacco products completely.

Statistics show that adult smoking rates have been cut nearly in half between 1965 and 2002, from 42.4 percent to 22.5 percent, and per capita consumption of tobacco products has fallen more than half, from 4,345 cigarettes in 1963 to 1,979 cigarettes in 2002. Perhaps these statistics prove that as a society we are trying to spread the message of nonsmoking, and if we continue to do so we will be well on our way to a healthier society.

Creating Social Change with Limited Corporate Support

The smoking issue is a prime example of social marketing at work. The Great American Smokeout made the issue top-of-mind for the nation and gave the public a call to action that reinforced the government's cigarette label warnings. The Great American Smokeout also was able to leverage considerable media attention in the early 1970s when the broadcast industry could no longer accept tobacco advertising. Since that time, there have been additional tobacco control laws aimed at defining where people cannot smoke (restaurants, public buildings, sports arenas, etc.) and keeping stronger tabs on the sale of tobacco to underage consumers. There have also been numerous industry-backed programs and campaigns ostensibly designed to reduce smoking among youth and sales of tobacco to underage consumers by retailers. All in all, the effect has been a significant reduction in smoking overall and a sustaining downward trend over the past few decades.

Anti-tobacco is also one of the few issues with limited appeal and success with respect to cause-related marketing. With the exception of the pharmaceutical industry, which has a substantial investment in research and product development to help people quit smoking and to treat patients with tobacco-related diseases (cancer, emphysema, chronic obstructive pulmonary disease or COPD, and others), other businesses are slow to provide visible support to the movement. Why is this the case when so many people are becoming disabled and dying from this behavior? One thought is that many of the companies you think would and should support the effort are concerned about losing key customers. Would a rental car company that prefers people not smoke in their cars come out to support the issue, knowing that one of their biggest corporate customers is a tobacco giant? How can a computer company go out on a limb when perhaps millions or even billions of dollars in hardware, software, and consulting service sales would be put in jeopardy? Think of all the other suppliers Altria, its divisions like Kraft Foods, and other tobacco companies use in the course of their businesses. It just makes sense that the issue will have to carry on without major corporate support.

PART III

CAUSE MARKETING PRACTICE

CHAPTER 10

BEST PRACTICES

A successful CRM campaign should rely upon certain principles, and they are described throughout this chapter.

1. *Obtain buy-in.*
Although the enthusiasm of the company's employees—especially those in charge of the partnership—is essential, the success of the relationship will likely depend on the support it receives from senior management and the CEO.

If you sense that senior management doubts the value of such an initiative, bringing in an outside consultant with expertise in CRM may help you win the support of key stakeholders by presenting a compelling case for the benefits that CRM will bring to your company. An outside consultant, additionally, can lend credibility and objectivity to the initiative.

Have senior management attend important meetings between you and the nonprofit group. Not only will this help to create buy-in, it will prepare your executives to speak eloquently about the partnership to the media and the community.

Your company spokesperson should be skilled in public speaking and other relevant skills to make sure he or she can effectively communicate the benefits of the CRM partnership to key constituents. Consider offering training if this person is uncomfortable or lacks the requisite expertise.

2. *Appoint a program champion.*
All successful CRM programs share a common characteristic: an executive at the corporation who is willing to take ownership of the program. This is equally true for NPs: your partnering firm needs to appoint an individual to manage the relationship.

Examples of individuals who typically fulfill this role at a corporation include the communications coordinator, the marketing director, and the company's president. If your firm lacks sufficient resources to appoint an individual to manage the relationship, consider hiring an outside professional. Usually, the executive director or communications coordinator at the nonprofit will be your counterpart.

3. Keep your senior management abreast of developments.
Regular communications noting significant achievements and potential obstacles will help keep management informed about the health of the partnership—something that should engender continued support.

As part of these communications, make sure that senior management learns about the accomplishments of the individuals behind the campaign. Recognition of employees should spur your team to even greater heights—and lets your executive team know that the CRM partnership is realizing tangible benefits.

4. Measure and communicate results.
The launch of a CRM program is the most difficult part of the process, as everything is new in the relationship. Therefore, it is key that everyone at the senior level of the company knows about the launch event and that the activities are featured in the press and communications. In addition, pairing their efforts with a celebrity spokesperson and the president of the nonprofit is key. The next question everyone will ask is measurement. How many eyeballs will see this campaign? Have a web plan tracker, a media tracker, a PSA report for radio and television, and a report for every key influencer that looked at the program.

CRM requires buy-in at a senior level with seasoned professionals who have a consistency of reach and revenue with CRM for their brands. Some good examples of programs and the executives that launched them follow.

- Jim O'Connell of Procter & Gamble (P&G) launched many successful relationships and established the importance of marketers who can execute and deliver results. For example, the President's Council on Physical Fitness and Sports's (PCPFS) multibrand, freestanding insert program reached 54 million homes and gave away a booklet designed with the National Fitness Leaders Association called "Looking Good Basics." There is continuity in that Melissa Johnson, a contributor to the booklet, is now the executive director at the PCPFS. P&G did many more successful, promotions, including the National Home Safety Test to benefit the National Safety Council. This was executed to 54 million consumers. O'Connell then successfully headed the Brand Savers Program for P&G with causes such as Susan G. Komen and the AHA.

P&G has been a pioneer in CRM. The significance of its efforts is that they are supported by the power brands and featured as an event in retail stores. Crest, Scope, Tide, Ivory, Olay, Sure, and Noxzema are part of the marketing mix. Kroger, Wal-Mart, Safeway, and Walgreens are part of the execution.

- Shawn Dennis, head of Global Corporate Branding for MasterCard, contributed to pioneering co-branded credit cards with causes such as the American Heart Association, American Cancer Society (ACS), and the Humane Society of the United States (HSUS). MasterCard made a significant financial commitment to co-branding and gave money to nonprofits for CRM. MasterCard's core banks—MBNA, Chase, and Citi—also followed its lead with heavy financial support.

- International Dairy Foods Association's (IDFA) Kurt Greitzer proved he was a pioneer marketer by allowing the heart-check symbol on 6 billion cartons of milk produced by nearly 2,500 independent dairies.

- The leadership of Brock Leach and Steve Rineman of PepsiCo created a very successful program with the Smart Spot brand and America on the Move. Brock continues his leadership by executing AOM with the National Council of La Raza and the National Urban League. PepsiCo's Smart Spot was significant because it required the brands to reformulate their fat and nutritional contents. This was a bold move for PepsiCo that has paid off with big results.

- CRM marketing legend Harry Abel forged the relationship between the Arthritis Foundation and Johnson & Johnson's Tylenol brand. Together they launched the easy-open top designed for people with arthritis and explored Tylenol/AF co-branding. This increased brand share and created a new and innovative remodel of a powerhouse brand. The Johnson & Johnson arthritis packaging was unique and significant to the consumer products industry as it recognized a group with special needs that was a valuable consumer segment.

• Tony DeLio of Archer Daniels Midland partnered healthy eating with his soy brands, heart-check, and the American Heart Walk. This benefited consumers who needed healthy lifestyle choices while creating walkers, walk teams, and money for the AHA. ADM's commitment was significant because the whole budget of its soy group was based on the AHA partnership.

• Elise Leong, MCI president, leveraged with the Magic Johnson Foundation with Towalame Austin by successfully partnering with the History Makers Education in 2005. History Makers has made significant accomplishments and is associated with an important movement to the African American community. The Magic Johnson Foundation is truly a representative of this effort through its 21 technology centers. MCI's commitment to the Magic Johnson Foundation and History Makers was significant because it invested major marketing dollars in African American youth.

Best Practices for a Successful CRM Program

So what are best practices that companies use when creating and measuring CRM campaigns? And how do they build an ongoing, compelling business case that proves that partnership is worth the investment?

1. *Alignment with business goals.*
Although many companies have an altruistic streak, they exist, first and foremost, to generate profits. The relationship between the corporation and the nonprofit, as well as the subsequent strategies and tactics that are implemented, must align with the company's business goals and yield tangible results.

• Cheerios put a heart-check on its packaging and marketed a heart-shaped cereal bowl as a consumer incentive, which

increased their share by 4 percent during a cereal war. The
company helped consumers eat better and feel better while
promoting a great cause.

- Comcast donated $50 million worth of TV time to the
  Partnership for a Drug Free America and leveraged their
  corporate social responsibility at the same time.
- Susie Upton and Kathy Rogers demonstrated their vision by
  promoting the Red Dress Campaign with sponsors Pfizer and
  Federated Department Stores, which was executed by Ronnie
  Taft of Federated.

2. *Opportunities for recognition.*
CRM programs that enjoy sustained enthusiasm with employees
are ones that include opportunities for recognition. Individuals
involved with the program typically like to receive praise for their
efforts.

3. *Engaging employees.*
Companies that are serious about their CRM initiatives engage the
workforce in the effort. They encourage employees to live the
values of the partnership and to take concrete actions that bring
these values to life.

- Allstate rewards its best salesmen with the Good Hands
  Program, which ties in several causes.
- Cendant rewards its division with a commitment to After
  School All Stars.
- Walgreens rewards its employees who perform and compete
  with programs sponsored by the AHA and the ACS.
- Avon recognizes and rewards its employees with their three-day
  Breast Cancer event.
- ING and Duane Reade show employee recognition by
  participating in the New York City Marathon.

4. *Capitalizing on company expertise.*
CRM partnerships that really take off are ones that leverage a
company's core competencies and are extensions of its areas of
expertise. It would make no sense for a furrier to partner with an
animal rights group, but a chemical manufacturer trying to clean

up its facilities would enhance its image by partnering with an
environmental organization.

- In order to sell records, every year Target picks a charity with
  leading celebrities and sells over 5 million copies of a
  customized compilation album with $1 per album contributed
  to the cause.
- Medtronic partners with the AHA to further their heart disease
  business.
- Ronald McDonald Children's charities helps McDonald's sell
  more hamburgers and fries.
- Blockbuster rents more videos with its Reading Is Fundamental
  literacy program.
- Kitchen Aid sells dishwashers focusing on breast cancer and the
  Susan G. Komen Foundation.
- Estée Lauder gets the attention of women with the Breast
  Cancer Research Foundation.
- Pharmaceutical manufacturers of psychiatric drugs get a
  lift by partnering with the National Mental Health
  Association.
- Florida Department of Citrus sells more orange and grapefruit
  juice by partnering with the AHA, the ACS, and the March of
  Dimes health causes.
- Paul Newman helps healthy eating with his products and gives
  money to his charities.
- Sting helps the rainforest with his music and leverages many
  corporations to the issue.

5. *Make cause marketing strategic.*
As successful programs have proven, CRM initiatives must
become a strategic component of corporate planning and must
have support of senior management. The overall marketing
program of the brand must be integrated. For instance, Unilever's
Dove brand is positioned as supporting the natural beauty that is
in every woman, therefore a relationship with America on the
Move would work incredibly well as the organization's core
"customer" is "Jayne," a working woman between 35-55 and
Unilever's bull's-eye target.

6. *Make corporate giving, CRM, and corporate social responsibility key brand values.*

Companies that fail to demonstrate genuine concern for social issues, or give lip service to it, may be viewed as cynical and manipulative. Brand building is core to nonprofits and corporations. Consistency for the brands comes from key messages and what is referred to as "relationship statements." A relationship must exist between the consumer and the brand promise. Dove in its new campaign says beauty is for everyone. They need a cause or issue such as America on the Move's "small steps" approach to help everyone attain and maintain a healthy weight. As a result of the nonprofit's credibility with respect to the issue, it is now Unilever's opportunity to promote vitality with an America On the Move partnership.

7. *Involve the whole organization.*

Although you need a program champion, you also need the active participation of the entire organization. Timberland's ten-year relationship with City Year is a wonderful example of a company that has a program champion that has all its employees involved in its CRM efforts. In managing its partnership with City Year, Timberland not only leverages the expertise of its social enterprise staff, but also solicits input from its CEO and communications, marketing, and human resources departments. Timberland also encourages its employees to become involved through regular organizational meetings and events, internal company communications, and paid leave for community service.

8. *Plan globally, engage locally.*

Companies need to be mindful of how their activities around the globe affect various local cultures. If a company is operating a manufacturing plant in Southeast Asia, for instance, it needs to know not only the rules governing import-export and monetary exchange rates, but how its operations affect the community— and then take steps to make sure that it is a good corporate citizen.

Instead of being reactive, as in the above example, companies should be proactive, looking for social causes they can champion.

Not only can this build goodwill with workers and the community-at-large, but it also can avoid offending Western consumers who don't want to buy products produced in sweatshops or prison labor camps.

For example, Kathy Lee Gifford and her affiliation with her charities made her reactive to this exact issue. As a result, she gave much of her free time to the Partnership Against Child Abuse.

If senior management needs to be convinced of the worth of the CRM partnership, it is wise for the program's corporate champion to gather data on anticipated impacts. Consumers, for instance, say that a company's support of social issues is an important element when making key community, employment, purchasing, and investment decisions, such as

- which companies they want to see doing business in their community.
- where they want to work.
- which products and services they use or would recommend to others.
- which stocks/mutual funds they would invest in.

On the other hand, the wrong decision can prompt negative response by the community, including

- switching to other corporate products or services.
- condemning the company in conversations with friends and family.
- refusal to invest in the firm.
- boycotting the company's products or services.
- causing confusion with stakeholders, including employees, investors, and the press.

For instance, brands that are not eco-friendly can lose market share, lose revenue, and alienate loyalists. Brands that are not pet-friendly lose an important marketing metric, while brands that are pet-friendly gain share. For instance, Mars, in its support of animal shelters and the HSUS, gained share support and press.

Chapter 10 • Best Practices   109

Carefully conceived and well-implemented, effective CRM programs can enhance a company's credibility, differentiate it and its brand from competitors, strengthen the relationship between the company and its key stakeholders, and have a positive effect on its bottom line.

Identifying the Right Issue or Cause

Although any number of issues might be a potential candidate for a CRM relationship, smart companies seek relationships that are aligned with their products/services, key demographic segments, and geography. The savviest companies go a step further to see how the cause meshes with their strategic business goals.

For instance, a company seeking to ensure a future labor pool of well-educated workers might choose to commit to an education-related organization or cause that helps young people at risk of falling behind academically or dropping out of school.

Also important to a CRM program is audience. What are the demographics and psychographics of each group? For instance, if you are focusing on women, the cause might be the AHA's America on the Move program. If you are focusing on men, you might partner with the Prostate Cancer Foundation or Alzheimer's Foundation. If you are looking for a warm and fuzzy, you might choose children's charities such as Save the Children or Empower Peace. If you want a pet charity, you could pick the HSUS or the ASPCA.

Demographics, psychographics, and buying power are the keys to success.

Benchmarking: Quantitative Criteria

Benchmarks should be created to determine the effectiveness of the program. Quantitative ones might include money raised to support the cause, enhanced customer loyalty to products, penetration of new market segments, and increased sales. Consider conducting consumer surveys to determine if the campaign is changing buying habits, increasing the visibility of the product, extending the brand, and so forth.

When considering a potential program name for a new health program directed toward men, the America Urology Association asked Charity Brands to conduct consumer research to ensure we would not alienate any population groups. The budget did not allow for extensive, customized research, so we opted to include questions in one of the many omnibus surveys implemented by research companies. Within a matter of days, and at a cost of about a thousand dollars, we were able to verify that our proposed theme was meaningful to the audience and would not alienate them.

CRM efforts also should improve employee productivity and cut employee turnover. Work with your HR department to do a "before and after" comparison of employee turnover and other surveys that measure morale. Also try to determine if the CRM is resulting in enhanced productivity.

Many employees participate in walks, runs, and marathons that benefit their companies' selected charities. Employee morale grows by meeting coworkers and partnering organizations. Live examples are Walgreens, Target, CVS, Duane Reade, Kmart, and Wal-Mart in the drug and discount category. Each of these companies makes room for employees and CRM.

Benchmarking: Qualitative Criteria

Qualitative criteria are more subjective and can include informal consumer or employee feedback, testimonials from individuals who have benefited from the partnership, company events, and employee recognition. But qualitative criteria can be as valuable as quantitative criteria, for they can be repurposed in a company's corporate communications.

Work with your media department (or public relations firm) to gain the maximum benefit from testimonials and employee feedback. Examples of this include

- Issuing press releases about success stories to relevant media outlets
- Encouraging reporters to write human interest stories about individuals benefiting from the CRM partnership
- Using quotes from individuals who have benefited from the CRM partnership on the company's website and in the annual report and other corporate collateral
- Putting employees' quotes on the company's website to attract new hires or to demonstrate the company's philanthropic activities

These qualitative tactics can be quantified, and the results can be impressive and compelling. Use the following formula to measure the value of your public relations initiative:

1. Find out the ad rates for the newspapers, magazines, television, and radio programs that run your story.
2. Measure the length of your piece.
3. Multiply (or divide) the length of your piece by the ad rate to determine the value of the placement.

While this formula won't measure intangibles such as goodwill, it will let your company determine the monetary value of media placements. And this information can be effective in convincing key stakeholders at your company that the CRM partnership is yielding real benefits.

Using Celebrity Involvement to Create Awareness and Address Challenges

Celebrities walk and drink champagne. Celebrities can enhance visibility, engender credibility, and attract the media's attention to CRM campaigns. It's no secret, though, that some of these individuals can be very demanding and difficult. What follows are some tips you can use for selecting and managing a celebrity spokesperson.

When selecting a celebrity partner, first put yourself in this individual's shoes and ask, "What's in it for me?"

Celebrities get involved in CRM campaigns for a variety of reasons. Some care about the cause; some want to be paid; some want media exposure; some want to improve their image. When the monetary "carrot" is unavailable, dangle some of these other ones to convince a celebrity to join the cause.

Now that you've partnered with the celebrity spokesperson, determine how much time he or she can give to the cause. Be considerate and appreciative of the celebrity's time, for the more popular the celebrity, the less time he or she will likely have for you. Ensure that the time the celebrity does give to a cause makes a difference, and make as few demands upon him or her as possible.

Prior to a media opportunity, make a list of talking points and "frequently asked questions" that cover everything this individual will need to know. You also should provide a detailed itinerary for every media event: arrival time, the name and personality of the interviewer, the questions that will be asked, suggested answers, departure time, and so forth. Help the individual feel secure and confident about media opportunities by covering every detail and providing answers to all possible questions.

If you need to talk to your celebrity spokesperson before an event, keep it short and try to handle it by phone, fax, or email. Don't ask for a one-on-one meeting unless it is essential. If you have to meet, try to keep the appointment to less than an hour. When you do meet, don't overload him or her with facts and figures. Identify three or four key points that you want your celebrity to communicate to the media.

There are some caveats that come with working with high-profile celebrities that you must keep in mind before targeting the best spokesperson for your cause. They are

1. Will the celebrity show up?
2. What will the celebrity say?
3. What is the spokesperson contracted to do and for how long?
4. What does the celebrity cost?
5. What do the spokesperson's agents and publicists allow with regard to endorsements and appearances in support of nonprofit organizations?

Finally, don't make any promises you can't keep, and keep all of the promises you make. If you fail to do this, you will find it difficult to get this—or another—celebrity to help with your CRM efforts.

Follow the rules in this chapter carefully, and work with a checklist. Seize the opportunities for reach and revenue in the next chapter. Opportunities are as good as the day of press, the day of market integration, launch, and the powers of both the nonprofit and consumer brands.

CHAPTER 11

OPPORTUNITIES IN CAUSE LICENSING

Cause Licensing—A Powerful Way to Drive Sales

Cause licensing refers to using a brand or trademark with a product to benefit a cause. A popular arrangement that corporations and non-profits use in CRM campaigns—and an outgrowth of CRM—cause licensing is a proven tactic that works. Specifically, it involves a for-profit firm (the licensee) using the equity of a nonprofit organization (the licensor) to create a link between the sale of the licensed product and the cause. The purpose of this type of arrangement is to increase sales for the licensee by leveraging the brand equity of the nonprofit and to generate donations and revenues for the licensor.

For instance, the Humane Society of the United States has a cata-log with its logos on products, the American Heart Association licenses its heart-check logo on billions of food products, and UNICEF licenses its name on greeting cards. The Live Strong bracelet is an example of a licensed item and platform fueled by Nike.

Aside from selling UNICEF's holiday cards at IKEA locations and donating 100 percent of the proceeds to UNICEF, a venture that has brought the charity $2.1 million dollars since 1988, the partnership also produced the IKEA Brum bear in 2003 to benefit UNICEF. Two dollars from the sale of every $6.99 bear were donated to support the charity's programs for children affected by war.

The American Red Cross and Ty Beanie Babies provide another mutually beneficial cause-licensed partnership. Ty began selling the blue "America" bear, a tribute to the memory of 9/11 in October 2001, and it has since generated more than $1.1 million for the American Red Cross Disaster Relief Fund. As a result of the success of the first "America" bear, in February 2002, Ty introduced a second edition "America" bear in order to honor American Red Cross chap-ters that provide lifesaving services and education in local communities year-round.

Companies and nonprofits are flocking to the cause-licensing model because it allows them to boost sales without having to make any significant investment or to develop new corporate strategies. It is, simply put, an easy, effective, and powerful solution. Companies continue to manufacture, market, and sell their products but add one additional step: They overtly support the nonprofit's mission and promote the partnership in advertising materials by using the real estate of the product's packaging.

As shown in Chapter 2, a recent survey revealed that 78 percent of consumers stated, "I'd be more likely to buy a product supporting a cause"; and that 62 percent would "pay more for a product that supports a cause" (The 2004 Cone Corporate Citizenship Study, Boston, MA).

The conclusion is clear and compelling: Cause licensing is an efficient and effective tool for boosting a company's sales.

Benefits for Nonprofits

Cause licensing also is an attractive proposition for nonprofits, for they receive increased funds through the sale of the licensed product or service. Nonprofits particularly like this arrangement because licensing agreements tend to result in larger revenue streams than one-time corporate charitable donations.

Placing a nonprofit's logo on a consumer product, which is part of a cause-licensing program, also tends to build brand awareness for the philanthropic institution, yet another added benefit that can translate into additional support. A common example of this is the Center for Missing and Exploited Children's family-oriented causes found on milk cartons. This relationship helps bring home some of the approximately 800,000 children that are reported missing each year.

Smaller Firms and Cause-Licensing Programs

For many CRM initiatives to succeed, they require corporations and nonprofits that have national or international reach, significant resources, and clout. Smaller firms, however, can enjoy some of the same benefits as their larger counterparts—especially because cause-licensing programs require a comparatively small investment of capital and resources.

The Body Shop supported a battered women initiative with a small budget by instituting a cell phone trade-in program. Hugo Boss and

Esquire magazine supported the prostate cancer issue by participating in the Blue for Men campaign. Sephora supports Operation Smile. These are all retail programs with little new budget investment, but just cause licensing overall.

The key point here is that cause licensing may be an ideal strategy for companies and nonprofits of all sizes—an initiative that drives sales of products and enhances brand awareness for both parties.

Forging Cause-Licensing Partnerships

Cause-licensing partnerships must begin with some market analysis. If a marketplace is flooded with cause-licensing partnerships, you may wish to look for other, more promising arenas. And if you choose to enter a crowded marketplace, you must craft a strategy that will enable you to stand above your competitors.

One way of cutting through the cause-licensing clutter is to partner with nonprofits that can lift the sales of your products and services. A way to determine if your partner can do this is to ask the following question: "Will the nonprofit give my company access to new constituents or capture the attention of the existing customer base?"

Even in a crowded market, a nonprofit with considerable cachet can still help a product rise above the fray. Assume a toy company is trying to increase its market share and is likely to be competing with icons such as Mickey Mouse, Dora the Explorer, Sponge Bob, and so forth. But a licensing partnership with Save the Children could give the firm the boost it needs to gain some traction in the marketplace. Save the Children and the kids who are supported by the cause become the cause-licensing celebrity, generating substantial reach and revenue for the cause. An example of this strategy is Denny's selling Save the Children ties.

Create and prioritize potential cause-licensing agreements by using the following three criteria:

1. Forge cause-licensing agreements in marketplaces that have few or none.
2. If this is not possible, seek a partner with enough cachet to give your product a lift above the competition.
3. If this is not possible, select a cause-licensing effort for a product/service in a less crowded field.

A Cause-Licensing Success Story

An excellent example of a company that both enhanced a tarnished corporate image and increased sales of a product line through cause licensing is The Home Depot. Once attacked for cutting down old-growth trees for its products, The Home Depot stopped this practice and forged a partnership with the National Wildlife Federation to create products such as birdfeeders and birdseed packaging for the joint "Backyard Wildlife Sanctuary" initiative.

As a result of this program, global retail sales of licensed products were 172 billion and there were $5.8 billion in royalties.

Spontaneity and Flexibility Also Are Key

Although many cause-licensing programs are the result of careful research, some just seem to occur serendipitously. Defined here, serendipity is the ability of a corporate executive to spot an opportunity overlooked by his or her associates and act immediately.

For example, the Women's Tennis Association started training Special Olympic athletes and Bergdorf Goodman did a fashion show for the athletes. Olympian attendees included Chris Evert, Gabrielle Sabatini, and Steffi Graf.

In summary, an organization must perform due diligence when searching for a partner, be aware enough to seize opportunities that suddenly appear, and then have the market insight and savvy to create licensing arrangements that will drive sales. Although this may seem burdensome, cause-licensing initiatives can provide your company and your nonprofit partner with increased revenue streams, enhanced brand awareness, and goodwill for many years.

From the Perspective of Nonprofits

Before entering into a cause-licensing agreement, nonprofits should develop a list of corporations that have similar interests, missions, and values. The nonprofit organization needs to understand the marketplace in which the company competes. The accompanying challenges and opportunities, as well as how the partnership can help both parties capitalize on these opportunities must also be understood.

Implicit in this is that executives at the nonprofit will have at least a rudimentary understanding of how its partner operates, the nuances and peculiarities of the industry, terminology, and so forth.

As your organization's reputation is entering a very public arena, you need to be knowledgeable about the marketplace, sales potential, risks, and so on. And you also want to enter cause-licensing agreements that will help you accomplish your goals.

In order to maximize revenues, nonprofits should then follow the same three guidelines enumerated below when selecting a corporation and forming a cause-licensing agreement:

1. Forge cause-licensing agreements in marketplaces that have few or none.
2. If this is not possible, seek a partner with enough cachet to give your product a lift above the competition.
3. If this is not possible, select a cause-licensing effort for a more promising product/service.

A Few More Tips for Nonprofits

As much as a corporation may need to convince you of the benefits that you will enjoy as a result of the partnership, you will need to sell the corporation on the strength of your organization. Be clear about what you can bring to the partnership. And don't expect the corporation to do all of the work.

Don't fall in love with your partner and forgo appropriate legal consultation. Your prospective partner is likely to have access to legal counsel, but you should probably have your own independent counsel to help draft a non-negotiable, boilerplate contract.

Challenges and Pitfalls

Cause licensing obviously brings many benefits: increased sales, greater brand awareness, increased goodwill, differentiation of your product from competitors, and enhanced consumer loyalty. But inherent in any venture that holds real rewards are significant risks, pitfalls, and challenges.

Use the following list to help uncover potential issues before they become intractable problems.

- Determine in advance what product categories, licensees, and/or distribution channels are off-limits, and respect these decisions.
- Develop your own ethical criteria for potential partners, and do not deviate from your values.
- Perform the necessary due diligence to determine if a corporate partner is a good match.
- Find people at your partner organization with whom you can collaborate.

A Cause-Licensing Failure

The American Medical Association (AMA)/Sunbeam debacle of 1997 stands as a stern warning to organizations that fail to adhere to the above guidelines.

In 1997, the AMA agreed to endorse healthcare products made by Sunbeam in return for financial support in the form of millions of dollars. But many AMA members dropped their membership in protest because they considered the partnership to be an inappropriate commercial arrangement that violated the organization's spirit and role as an objective voice. This mass outcry and defection eventually forced the AMA to void the contract. Insisting that the AMA honor the contract or pay damages for breach of contract, Sunbeam sued, and the failed deal cost the AMA an estimated $16 million.

The lesson here can be seen in the failure to follow guidelines: Both parties did not to determine if the channel was an appropriate one for a cause-licensing arrangement (guideline #1), and then violated the ethical underpinnings of the membership (guideline #2).

Another Cause-Licensing Success Story

In contrast, the following story clearly illustrates the significant benefits both parties receive from this arrangement.

Charity Brands helped the AHA in 1995 establish the Food Certification Program—an initiative that provided consumers with a quick and easy way to identify heart-healthy foods. The now famous heart-check logo, a centerpiece of the program, is now licensed by more than 90 companies for more than 500 products.

How did the AHA avoid the problems that plagued the AMA and Sunbeam? How was a perceived conflict of interest avoided? Why was the relationship a success?

At the start of the program, it was decided that products displaying the AHA heart-check logo had to meet stringent nutritional guidelines and pass a thorough review process conducted by AHA medical researchers. This simple but powerful decision enlisted influential thought leaders at the AHA and gained their tacit approval, which in turn allayed the concerns of members of potentially improper business relationships. These simple steps generated widespread support for the partnership, allowing it to flourish and enabling multiple parties to realize significant benefits.

Cause Licensing and Affinity Credit Cards

Affinity credit cards—cards that feature a nonprofit's name and logo that are marketed to individuals interested in that organization—have become a popular vehicle for cause licensing.

Affinity credit cards offer numerous benefits for a nonprofit by

- Providing an incremental revenue stream that supports the organization's mission and activities
- Providing a source of guaranteed revenue
- Enhancing customer loyalty among the nonprofit, its members, the card issuer, customers, and other core constituents
- Creating awareness of the organization's activities through monthly card statements

Examples of successful affinity card programs abound. MBNA Credit Cards and The Nature Conservancy; NBNA; and First Bank, Citibank, and other major financial institutions have issued hundreds of affinity cards that have generated millions of donations for nonprofits, such as the World Wildlife Federation, the American Red Cross, and Save the Children.

Our experience has been that checks, credit cards, address labels, and online shopping are a few examples of low hanging fruit in the world of nonprofit licensing. Typically banks look for large affinity groups with large databases and pay dearly for that access. Visa and MasterCard also participate with healthy and charity messages, prizes, incentives, and special offers to create volume. The affinity marketing now permeates all brands of insurance as well.

Summing It Up

Cause licensing is one of the most effective tools in a marketer's arsenal and should be leveraged to the fullest. When done properly, both the company and the nonprofit will see significant benefits: increased sales and donations, product differentiation, enhanced goodwill, and much more.

Just follow the guidelines and tips described in this chapter to ensure that you forge an appropriate and effective cause-licensing agreement—and then enjoy the fruits of your labors.

CHAPTER 12

THE CHARITY BRANDS MARKETING MONITOR AND INDEX

For many years I have thought a measurement tool was needed to help corporations and nonprofits planning and/or evaluating philanthropic and CRM relationships and programs. While there is no substitute for due diligence, there are ways to make completing due diligence easier, faster, and more accurate. That is why I, as one of the first to specialize in this area, created the Charity Brands Marketing Index and Monitor, a tool that can be used by either party in the relationship to begin looking directionally and specifically for potential partners.

The tool has two parts:

The *CBM Corporate Giving Index* is designed to enable nonprofits to identify corporations that meet their requirements and plans for sponsorship and CRM programs by providing relevant information about major corporations and nonprofits on an ongoing basis—for example, their philanthropic giving and correlated business trends. The Index also indicates how a company's philanthropic and cause-related efforts affect shareholder value by overlaying a historical share price timeline to the company's visible CRM and corporate social responsibility activities.

The *CBM Cause-Related Marketing Monitor* is designed to help corporate executives identify nonprofit organizations that meet their marketing, human resources, and/or foundation needs (i.e., for reach through CRM, volunteerism opportunities for employees, and philanthropic support) by providing up-to-date information about organizations' mission, constituent reach, programming, sponsorship levels and benefits, etc. Similar to the Index, the Monitor enables nonprofit organizations to view other nonprofits to see how they can create more relevant programs and opportunities to attract corporate support.

Indexing both sectors under multiple criteria also facilitates

- Analysis of a potential corporate partner's social responsibility activities and business ramifications to ensure compatibility with the NP's mission and culture.
- Analysis of a potential nonprofit partner's stature among similar organizations and in the minds of the general consumer audience to establish the organization's "value" as a marketing property that can provide a rich return on investment.
- Analysis of the potential to create meaningful CRM relationships by leveraging the assets of companies and organizations reviewed.
- Evaluation of existing CRM program success, which can be used as a broad indicator for companies' and nonprofits' effectiveness and commitment to their marketing partners.

Both the Index and Monitor are updated quarterly in keeping with the fast pace of change that occurs in the world of CRM and corporate social responsibility. We announce top-line quarterly findings through general and industry-specific news media (e.g., retailing, philanthropy, packaged goods, financial, manufacturing, etc.), while the full report is packaged as a "subscription" product for both corporations and nonprofits. The Index and Monitor are also valuable for corporations and nonprofits that want to keep abreast of changes and opportunities offered by their competitors.

Much of the information included is typically available in corporations' and nonprofits' annual reports. Additional data is routinely announced to the media or easily obtained through interviews, syndicated research, etc. More specific data requires primary research interviews conducted directly with corporate and nonprofit leaders. Conducting, analyzing, indexing, formatting, and releasing the research on a quarterly basis for corporate and nonprofit marketers is a daunting task, yet it yields a truly valuable tool that I believe expands CRM and corporate social responsibility programs and opportunities for nonprofits and corporations alike.

The Index initially focuses on the ten largest U.S. corporations as measured by total corporate/corporate foundation giving, and correlates the direct (linear or nonlinear) relationship between the annual total giving and annual sales, stock price, and press mentions. The Index focuses on the direction, rather than the strength, of the relationship, yielding valuable information on

- enhanced corporate reputation
- effect of partnerships with nonprofits
- area(s) or issues supported by the corporation

The methodology enables us to rank the ten subject corporations on the identified parameters implicitly and focus on establishing the fact that benefits realized by corporate partners in CRM relationships outweigh the cost incurred. I also look directionally at the relationship between cost and benefits over a three- to five-year span. The end result is interesting, to say the least, for everyone involved in marketing and nonprofit management, and serves as a proven platform for expansion of the Index and Monitor project to include many more companies and nonprofit organizations.

Methodology

Most data is collected through secondary sources as noted above. Additional data requires conducting interviews, surveys, etc., directly with corporations and nonprofit organizations to ensure the ability to provide deep information accurately in reporting each entry.

We analyze the data for corporations and nonprofits as follows, and format the report with charts and graphs to help comprehension and comparison of the written descriptions of findings.

Corporations

- Annual corporate cash contributions, 1-year change, 5-year trend
- Annual corporate foundation contributions, 1-year change, 5-year trend
- Annual in-kind contributions, 1-year change, 5-year trend
- Annual contributions of employee time, 1-year change, 5-year trend
- Sales, 5-year trend
- Share Value, 5-year trend

- Employee Volunteerism, 5-year trend
- Employee growth, 5-year trend

The listing for Fannie Mae, a private, shareholder-owned company that works to make sure mortgage money is available for people in communities all across America, is found on the following page.

Each corporation is also ranked and indexed against all other corporations in the Index for total giving, sales trend, share value growth, and employee growth and volunteerism.

Nonprofits

- Annual corporate cash donations, # sponsors, 1-year change, 5-year trend
- Annual corporate foundation donations, # sponsors, 1-year change, 5-year trend
- Annual in-kind donations, # sponsors, 1-year change, 5-year trend
- Annual volunteer hours, # sponsors, 1-year change, 5-year trend
- Unpaid media impressions, 5-year trend
- Paid media impressions, 5-year trend
- Population served, 5-year trend

Each nonprofit is ranked and indexed against all other nonprofits for total corporate revenue received, total number of sponsors, total unpaid impressions, total paid impressions, and total population served.

In addition to individual entry pages, corporate and nonprofit rankings and indexes are reflected on additional "listings" pages (i.e., for corporations: Total Corporate Giving, Sales Increase, etc.; for nonprofits: Total Corporate Revenue, Total Unpaid Impressions, Total Paid Impressions, etc.). These pages are instrumental in helping the users quickly identify their realm of possible partners based on their most important criteria.

Product Value

The CBM Corporate Giving Index and Cause-Related Monitor is an extremely valuable tool to help gauge the effects of corporate giving on vital business issues. Current data indicates that companies

Fannie Mae Giving 2003

Contribution Type	Value (all)	Issues	Causes/Projects	1-year growth	5-year trend
Cash (corp.)	N/A*	N/A*	N/A*	N/A*	N/A*
Cash (corp. foundation in millions)	$52,901	Affordable Housing, Education, Diversity Awareness	Boys and Girls Club, Smart Grant America, Nonprofit Roundtable of Greater Washington	+54.2%	+64.3%
Employee time (in total hours for all employees)	540,000 hours	Affordable Housing, Education, Diversity Awareness	Varied projects: housing, community enhancement, education	+4.65%	+21.62%
Total	$52,901 mil 540,000 hrs	----------	461 grants awarded	+%	+%

*Donations are all made through Fannie Mae Foundation

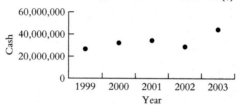

Foundation Cash Contributions ($)

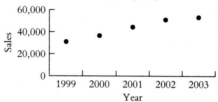

Sales ($mil)

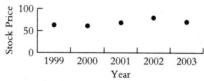

Average Stock Price ($)

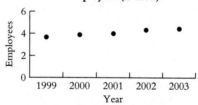

Employees (# thou)

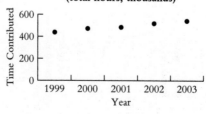

Employee Time Contributed
(total hours, thousands)

supporting causes that stakeholders care about have better performance in terms of

- Sales
- Investor attitudes
- Employee satisfaction and loyalty

Corporate giving may also significantly increase the number of positive mentions a company receives in the press over the course of a year.

The CBM Corporate Giving Index facilitates apples-to-apples comparisons on these business issues and helps corporate users quickly identify the social issues and nonprofit organizations supported by their business sector and their competitors to aid in strategic and tactical planning. The Index is also valuable for nonprofit organizations, as they strive to identify appropriate companies to approach with philanthropic requests and CRM proposals.

The CBM Cause-Related Marketing Monitor is valuable for users who want to identify potential nonprofit organizations for partnerships based on their effectiveness in generating consumer media impressions (paid and unpaid) and increasing their reach and services to constituents. Corporations looking for CRM partnerships typically want to know how prominent a nonprofit organization is in the marketplace, as more prominence usually means a better opportunity to leverage an organization's awareness, affinity, and credibility among consumers.

Companies are increasingly interested in how efficient organizations are with corporate revenue so they may claim "bragging rights" to helping an organization serve more people. The Cause-Related Marketing Monitor helps companies identify nonprofit organizations that

- Demonstrate efficiencies with respect to leveraging assets to reach more consumers and/or targeted individuals (e.g., healthcare professionals, educators, etc.).
- Fit their strategic and tactical plans for CRM programs/sponsorships.
- Facilitate an understanding of issues and organizations supported by their business sector and competitors.

Nonprofit organizations also find the Cause-Related Marketing Monitor is valuable for comparing its own CRM revenue and support to other organizations of similar size or addressing similar issues. I hope, and believe, that the end result of using the Index and Monitor over time will be a much more vibrant marketplace with corporations and nonprofits transacting business in huge numbers on a regular basis.

CHAPTER 13

BUILDING THE ACTION PLAN

Planning for a CRM program or campaign is not unlike planning for any other type of communications effort. You must first define your objectives, and then establish strategies and create tactics to meet the objectives within a specified timetable and budget. The difference when planning a CRM program is recognizing and leveraging the extraordinary range of opportunities and assets available to you and your nonprofit or corporate partner to utilize in meeting your mutual and individual goals. When you total up the combined communications assets of both parties, you will be surprised at how much the CRM relationship can be integrated into your existing marketing plans.

Since no two companies, brands, or nonprofits are exactly alike, there's little benefit in my suggesting hard and fast planning rules that might restrict your thinking during the development of a CRM relationship. I'd rather give you seven elements to explore and consider as a precursor to the planning effort. If you implement these basic suggestions, I'm confident you will uncover more than a few new ideas and assets that will enable you to have a much better program and an enjoyable personal experience along the way.

1. Identify the Right Partner

If you are considering CRM as a strategy for your company or nonprofit organization, you have probably already thought about the kind of organization or company that you'd like to have as your partner. But how do you know whether or not your top-of-mind candidate is right for you?

Consider the even broader expanse of opportunities that lay before you: How do you find the perfect partner from among the hundreds of thousands of companies and nonprofits in the U.S. alone, let alone the potentially millions of other possibilities worldwide?

I am sorry to tell you that there are few alternatives to due diligence. Finding and vetting the right organization or company for your partnership is probably the most basic element that is overlooked or omitted at the beginning of planning discussions. The first inclination is usually to partner with the biggest name in the field you are approaching, but sometimes the best partner isn't the biggest. Would American Express have the same clout with a better-known domestic hunger organization that it had with Share Our Strength? Would it have been able to achieve its marketing and contribution goals had it been hampered by another nonprofit's more restrictive policy? Who's to say? The point being that potential CRM partnerships offer an incredible number of options and alternatives, whether you're looking at it from the corporate or nonprofit side.

You may want to consider whether or not you're looking at the right issue or cause (if you are at a corporation) and whether you have your sights set on the right industry or corporation (if you are at a nonprofit) for the partnership you seek. What appears to be an ideal match may not always be your best choice, and something you think may be off-limits could potentially provide unlimited opportunity. Take the BMW/Komen Foundation example.

BMW thought it needed to approach women through the issue of heart disease. A relatively new issue, women and heart disease was in the media regularly, mostly because of the AHA's "Take Wellness to Heart" campaign. And although the AHA was high on BMW's list because of its size, reach, and reputation, the company ended up partnering with the Susan G. Komen Breast Cancer Foundation because Komen could accommodate its logistical needs.

Look at this same partnership from the Foundation's side. The Komen Foundation had a strong, visible relationship with Ford Motor Company as a national sponsor of its "Race for the Cure" events even while it had a high-level relationship with BMW (keep in mind that the relationship that went unknown and unexplored for quite some time became "The Ultimate Drive" program). But the Ford relationship made the Foundation take its eye off the auto industry as a source for additional corporate support. Once it became evident that the program being proposed by BMW would not conflict with the Ford agreement, the Foundation's eyes were opened to new possibilities for other programs with companies other than their existing event sponsors.

Significant time and effort are usually required to find and examine a partner that fits perfectly with your vision; one with the right measures of credibility and flexibility you need to establish your message. Phone calls, material reviews, third-party references, syndicated research, and in-person meetings all take time and effort . . . and that's all after you've identified the issues and causes to be considered. That alone can eat up valuable executive, staff, and/or consultant time, if you are really going about it strategically and not just exploring the most obvious potential partners or a "blue sky/what if" scenario.

It may be wise to engage an agency specializing in CRM to help you identify the appropriate corporation or nonprofit partner. The Internet has made due diligence somewhat easier, but it has also made us somewhat lax in scrutinizing the information we find.

A good specialist will have broad knowledge about how causes and corporations can best work together, and will also have in-depth knowledge about and contacts with many of the organizations and companies you may have under consideration. Using these outside capabilities can save you both time and money in the long run whether you are on the corporate or nonprofit side of the relationship.

2. Build the Relationship at the Top

Generally, the higher up your relationship goes, the better the resulting program or campaign. If the CEO or other leaders of the company and the nonprofit partner have a strong and vibrant relationship, you can count on more support internally, and potentially more resources down the road that will add support to the program and communication efforts. A strong-at-the-top relationship can also help ensure longevity as someone at the CEO or Executive VP level will have a better view of the "big picture" for a company or even an entire industry that will help sustain the partnership for the long term.

BMW/Komen Foundation notwithstanding, a strong relationship at the top is without question an effective way of integrating CRM throughout a brand's effort.

Take, for example, PepsiCo Smart Spot's sponsorship of America on the Move. This relationship was built at the very top of each organization's leadership. Dr. Jim Hill, co-founder of the nonprofit organization, worked directly with Brock Leach, the man leading PepsiCo's transition toward health and wellness. Together they have a view of what the nation is really craving and striving for with respect to physical activity, nutrition, and the benefits of good health. When America on the Move needed additional support for its national Day of Action campaign, Brock made sure PepsiCo was there doing all it could to support the organization and help the relationship provide an even greater return than anticipated by leveraging new opportunities that resulted in enormous media coverage nationally and locally.

The common vision among the two leaders also ensures the America on the Move relationship with Smart Spot will continue to drive mutual success. Great leaders understand that some things take more time than others to bear fruit. Once a personal commitment is made, they have enough confidence in their original assessment and strategic viewpoint to stay the course. Of course, that doesn't work at all levels of the corporate structure.

Too often, relationships are struck between a company and a nonprofit with the best intentions, but their development reflects a view of CRM as just another element in the marketing mix. This typically happens at the brand management level (rather than from a corporate marketing department), and is exactly the wrong way to approach an external partnership that can provide so much in terms of reach and revenue for both sides.

While many elements of a nonprofit's reach can be valued according to return on investment—for example, reach and visibility can be evaluated according to standard sponsorship criteria or traditional media calculations—often the value of a nonprofit brand and longevity of the corporate/nonprofit relationship is not taken seriously enough. This causes the development of performance criteria that allow little leeway, giving the sponsor an opportunity to drop the relationship after a year. The result is a lost marketing opportunity, wasted time and financial resources, a spate of negative feelings among the nonprofit's constituents, and questions about the brand's intentions in the first place.

I believe the backlash among the public and a nonprofit's constituents when a company supports a charity only briefly and appears to be serving only its own interests is not taken seriously enough. While most consumers understand a company's temporary or episodic support for a relief organization in times of disaster, companies that want to support healthcare, education, and underserved population issues are well advised to look further ahead than the next quarter's financial statement. If there is no long-term commitment, your audience will sniff you out, and credibility and support for both sides will be lost. The best way to make sure your effort is not subject to cancellation based on first-year results or the quarterly report is to create the higher-level relationship. My suggestion is to plan for success. If necessary, start smaller by developing and implementing a pilot effort, and then refine the program or campaign and roll it out with a greater level of confidence.

3. Do Something Unique and Sustainable—Creating Reach and Revenue for Your Brand

Nearly every CRM relationship can and should be unique, even if there are other sponsors supporting the same program. The uniqueness comes from the one-of-a-kind blend of two distinct and separate brands, the sponsoring company's and the nonprofit's. Even for companies in the same business, their approaches to the same nonprofit can support their own brands and industry positions. Think back to the example of the America Heart Association Pharmaceutical Round-table—more than a half-dozen major pharmaceutical companies supporting heart research and compliance education, and gaining access to and visibility among AHA's large professional constituency.

Several of the members were savvy enough to implement additional programs under their membership agreements. Bristol-Myers Squibb focused on risk assessment; Pfizer concentrated on cholesterol screenings. Both made measurable gains in awareness and recognition by leveraging the AHA relationship and did not conflict with the other's individualized and customized program.

Not too long ago, there were many successful "off-the-shelf" programs developed by major nonprofit organizations. A company would buy into a program, often to pre-empt competition from claiming the space through category exclusivity provisions in the contract. Initially, these programs often did well for the nonprofit and the corporate participants. But over time, the corporations tended to get lost in the "clutter of success"—having too many sponsors trying to share finite space and time. At that point, they needed to decide whether or not to give up the equity they had created for their category in the program, or drop out to better support their own brand equity and leave the category, which the program built, open for competition to swoop in. Now, communications technology and other market forces have enabled the narrowing of consumer targeting for commerce and social change, and many of these opportunities can be applied or added to the off-the-shelf programs and campaigns.

There are too many opportunities in the communications marketplace to rely solely on a one-size-fits-all charity/sponsor relationship. Some of those programs, which are primarily leftovers from the 1980s and 1990s, have adapted to the new 21st-century marketplace mentality, where the retailer is king and manufacturers now cater to the store owner or wait in line while the competition does. Some are at best languishing in invisibility. Many have gone by the wayside.

4. Pool Resources and Be Consistent in Your Approach

Think of the ways we receive marketing communications in an average day. How many telephone calls, brochures, catalogues, television commercials, newspaper ads, news articles in every media based on press releases, radio ads, clothing labels, vending machines, cell phone text messages, Internet pop-ups, emails, roadside signs, and store displays do you see in an average day? Looking at the sponsor/nonprofit relationship with a view toward strategic collaboration could potentially double the communications channels for both parties on any given project or campaign. What could that be worth in terms of reach and retention?

Think of all the ways you and your CRM partner communicate to your audiences. Consider the list on the previous page as just a start. If you can imagine a collaborative message that you both promote through all your respective channels, you'll have a much better chance of creating awareness, recognition, and action in light of the enormous number of messages every individual receives on a daily basis. Commit to using more of both partners' channels and see how much more effective your messaging can be.

5. Watch Out for Your Partner—Be a Good Co-Brand and Ally

Along with the breadth of opportunities in communications and cus-tomization of relationships comes some level of concern about branding identification, exclusivity, and audience access. The last thing you need to do is alienate your partner's constituents by requesting accommoda-tions that throw their credibility into question by the media, their loyal audience, or by a third party or group that is unintentionally offended. Both the corporation and the nonprofit need to regularly remind them-selves that their partner has the same concerns they do for their own image, message delivery, and budget/return on investment. Regular self-reminders along the way will help ensure development of a healthy relationship that does not hurt either the nonprofit's or the sponsor's brand.

Most potential pitfalls can be avoided simply by establishing basic ground rules at the very beginning of discussions. If you keep your ground rules to a minimum, you'll have a better chance of a fruitful discussion that leads to a program and relationship concept that will be successful for both parties. For example, many NPs are careful about triggering reaction in the media or among constituents about the "wrong kind of money" being contributed to the nonprofit or "too much of the wrong kind of spending" behind a program or campaign. But, as we see with the AHA and SUBWAY, there is a way to make re-lationship communications clear and plentiful, which fosters accept-ability among audiences of all types.

6. Be Ready for Marketplace Changes

As with any marketing endeavor, you must be cognizant, open, and responsive to change in the marketplace. Isn't it amazing how fast technologies and perceptions are developed and then adopted or abandoned? Even with an extraordinarily successful program, you need to keep not only abreast but ahead of marketplace changes to even maintain, let alone enhance, a CRM program or campaign. When a good thing becomes too good for one side of a CRM relationship, that side needs to look for a new component or strategy that can pro-pel them when the other side takes notice and wants or needs to change with the times.

Children's Miracle Network (CMN) had what may be considered the "mother of all cause-related Sunday newspaper freestanding insert programs"—at one point featuring more than 60 pages of coupon ads from consumer brands we all recognize. The program eventually found itself in jeopardy as a result of its own success; the participating brands realized they were being lost in an enormous amount of ads, all supporting this very worthy cause. Rather than succumbing to the peril of losing its manufacturer sponsors by adhering to its program model, CMN successfully solidified its supermarket, chain drug store, and mass merchandise retailer base supporting the program. This ensured continued support from manufacturers that wanted to be included in the in-store visibility components of the program, which are enormously important for sales. Their inclusion also gave them an additional reason and opportunity to discuss expanding their presence at retail through brand-specific promotions that benefit CMN. It is doubtful that CMN is resting on its haunches; no doubt it is looking at the next big development opportunity to keep it at the forefront of CRM in the U.S.

7. Help Your Partner Expand the Relationship

Try to open discussion and stimulate creative thinking to expand the CRM relationship to your other business partners. Opening doors for your primary nonprofit or corporate partner can help you in so many ways. For a nonprofit, it can lead to expanded visibility and revenue. For a corporate sponsor, enhanced trade relationships and credibility among, and interaction with, consumers can be created.

Here's one way crossing over to other business partners can work for CRM. Many manufacturers develop a selection of promotions that can be implemented by different retailers, helping each retailer tailor an in-store promotion that relates to a brand's advertising or promotional theme. So some develop the same type of "menu" program with a variety of promotional techniques that help a manufacturer's retailers leverage the CRM campaign for its particular audience or community. A few of the concepts developed for these types of menus include

- Co-branded merchandising that generates revenue for the retailer and the nonprofit.
- In-store or chainwide sweepstakes for a prize donated in-kind by another corporate sponsor.

- Custom-published magazine with content contributed by the nonprofit, the manufacturer, and the retail partner.
- Nonprofit signature or special event held in-store or in the parking lot.

So, there you have them, seven major elements to consider when beginning your CRM planning. You may not be able to incorporate all of them each time you pursue a program or campaign, but you will impress upon your partner or potential partner that you are thinking strategically about the relationship and giving the cooperative effort the best chance for success.

EPILOGUE

My journey into cause-related marketing has been a 20-year effort with lots of help from my colleagues and friends.

Ira Szot, our Chief Operating Officer, has shared his brilliance and bandwidth with hundreds of companies and all the major nonprofits. Emily Mack has been our leading star for over ten years, and Andrew Emmett and Kaylan Scagliola have jumped on the ship and made it successful. Herb Kozlov, of Reed Smith, has been a source of inspiration and carefully increased our strength and furthered our development.

The great news is that the budgets are getting bigger for CRM and corporate social responsibility—in the tens of millions to hundreds of millions of dollars. Every major company at the board level continues the journey with lots of energy, power, and branding. The boardrooms have become more concerned with how they are acting locally and thinking nationally and globally. The issues are being more defined. Education, hunger, health, men's rights, women's rights, all with more money and more entrepreneurial spirit. Companies are increasingly socially responsible and paying attention to the $1 trillion that the nonprofit sector generates from the boardroom to the broomroom.

STEPHEN M. ADLER
March 2006

BIBLIOGRAPHY AND REFERENCES

A Broken Promise to Our Children The 1998 State Tobacco Settlement Seven Years Later. November 30, 2005.

Adkins, Sue. *Cause Related Marketing: Who Cares Wins,* Oxford, UK: Butterworth-Heinemann, 2000.

Amery, Elizabeth A. "Creating Win-Win Relationships Through Cause-Related Marketing," *On Philanthropy.* June 11, 2001. <http://www.onphilanthropy.com/bestpract/bp2001-08-22i.html>

Blake, Connette. "Opportunities in Cause Licensing," *On Philanthropy.* June 18, 2004. <http://www.onphilanthropy.com/bestpract/bp2004-06-18.html>

Broon, Peggy Simcic and Albana Belliu Vriony. "Corporate Social Responsibility and Cause Related Marketing: An Overview," *International Journal of Advertising.* 2001.

Brown, David, Keeble, Justin, and Sarah Roberts, "The Business Case for Corporate Citizenship," Cambridge, UK: Arthur D. Little, Limited. <http://www.adlittle.uk.com/insights/articles/?id=13>

Byrne, John A. "The Man Who Invented Management—Why Peter Drucker's Ideas Still Matter," *Businessweek,* November 28, 2005: 97–106.

"Cause Related Marketing—Reaping the Benefits," 2004. <http://www.bitc.org.uk>

Cheng, Kipp. "New Numbers Make the Case: Ethnic Spending Power Continues Rapid Rise," *DiversityInc.com,* December 6, 2002. <http://www.aef.com/06/news/data/2002/2212>

Chronicle of Higher Education. March 18, 2005. Section: Students, Volume 51, Issue 28, Page A34

"Color Coded Causes," *Advertising Age,* June 13, 2005: 31–35.

Environmental Health Perspectives, VOLUME 113, NUMBER 8, August 2005.

Humphreys, Jeffery M. "The Multicultural Economy 2004: America's Minority Buying Power," *Georgia Business and Economic Conditions,* Volume 64, Number 3: 2004.

Irwin, Ron. "Can Branding Save the World?" April 8, 2002. <http://www.brandchannel.com>

Lamons, Bob. *The Case for B2B Branding Pulling Away from the Business-to-Business Pack,* Mason, OH: Thomson Learning, 2005.

Marconi, Joe. *Cause Marketing,* Chicago: Dearborn Trade Publishing, 2002.

Market Research on the Indian Market Place, a presentation by Susan Masten and J. D. Williams, Circumpolar Conference, 1996.

Meyer, Harvey. "When the Cause Is Just," *Journal of Business Strategy*, Nov/Dec. 1999: 27–31.

MichelMan, Paul. "Why Retention Should Become a Core Strategy Now," Harvard Management Update, October 2003.

Peoples, John C. "Diversity Practices That Work: The American Worker Speaks," *National Urban League.*

Sharing Solutions for Childhood Obesity. Environmental Health Perspectives, Volume 113, Number 8, August 2005

Steckel, Richard. *Making Money While Making a Difference,* Homewood, IL: High Tide Press Inc., 1999.

Market and Statistics Reports

"African American Market Profile," *Magazine Publishers of America*, 2004.

"Asian-American Market Profile," *Magazine Publishers of America*, 2004.

"Hispanic/Latino Market Profile," *Magazine Publishers of America*, 2004.

Cone/Roper Reports, 1999–2004 <http://www.coneinc.com>

"2004 American Community Survey," *U.S. Census Bureau.*

"Current Population Survey," *U.S. Census Bureau*, March 2005

The World Factbook <http://www.cia.gov/cia/publications/factbook>

Websites

American Heart Association <http://www.americanheart.org>
American Cancer Society <http://www.cancer.org>
American Diabetes Association <http://www.diabetes.org>
American Legacy Foundation <http://www.americanlegacy.org>
American Lung Association <http://www.lungusa.org>
Avon Foundation http://www.avonfoundation.org
Campaign for Tobacco Free Kids http://www.tobaccofreekids.org
The Cause Marketing Forum http://www.causemarketingforum.org
Center for Disease Control http://www.cdc.gov
Fannie Mae <http://www.fanniemae.com>
Fannie Mae Foundation <http://www.fanniemaefoundation.org>
Forbes.com—Forbes Top 500 1999–2003 <http://www.forbes.com>
The Human Rights Campaign <http://www.humanrights.org>

IKEA   <http://www.ikea-group.ikea.com/>

KaBoom!   <http://www.kaboom.org>

Lifetime Television   <http://www.lifetimetv.com>

The Centers for Disease Control and Prevention   <http://www.cdc.gov>

The Magic Johnson Foundation   <http://www.magicjohnson.org>

The Home Depot   <http://www.homedepot.com>

The National Council of La Raza   <http://www.nclr.org>

The National Urban League   <http://www.nul.org>

The Sierra Club   <http://www.sierraclub.com>

The Society for Non Profits   <http://www.snpo.org>

Wal-Mart   <http://www.walmartfoundation.org>

INDEX

About TEXERE

Texere, a progressive and authoritative voice in business publishing, brings to the global business community the expertise and insights of leading thinkers. Our books educate, enlighten, and entertain, and provide an intersection where our authors and our readers share cutting edge ideas, practices, and innovative solutions. Texere seeks to cultivate, enhance, and disseminate information that illuminates the global business landscape.

www.thomson.com/learning/texere

About the typeface

This book was set in 10.5/14pt Bembo. Bembo was cut by Francesco Griffo for the Venitian printer Aldus Manutius to publish in 1495 *De Aetna* by Cardinal Pietro Bembo. Stanley Morison supervised the design of Bembo for the Monotype Corporation in 1929. The Bembo is a readable and classical typeface because of its well-proportioned letterforms, functional serifs, and lack of peculiarities.

Library of Congress Cataloging-in-Publication Data

Adler, Stephen M.
   Cause for concern : results-oriented cause marketing / Stephen M. Adler.
     p. cm.
   Includes bibliographical references and index.
    ISBN 0-324-31130-3
  1. Social marketing. 2. Social responsibility of business. I. Title.

   HF5414.A353 2006
   658.8--dc22

2006013103